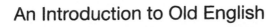

An Introduction to Old English

Edinburgh Textbooks on the English Language

General Editor
Heinz Giegerich, Professor of English Linguistics (University of Edinburgh)

Editorial Board
Laurie Bauer (University of Wellington)
Derek Britton (University of Edinburgh)
Olga Fischer (University of Amsterdam)
Norman Macleod (University of Edinburgh)
Donka Minkova (UCLA)
Katie Wales (University of Leeds)
Anthony Warner (University of York)

TITLES IN THE SERIES INCLUDE

An Introduction to English Syntax
Jim Miller

An Introduction to English Phonology
April McMahon

An Introduction to English Morphology
Andrew Carstairs-McCarthy

An Introduction to International Varieties of English
Laurie Bauer

An Introduction to Middle English
Simon Horobin and Jeremy Smith

An Introduction to Old English

Richard Hogg

Edinburgh University Press

© Richard Hogg, 2002

Edinburgh University Press Ltd
22 George Square, Edinburgh

Reprinted 2007, 2009

Typeset in Janson
by Norman Tilley Graphics and
printed and bound in Great Britain
by CPI Antony Rowe, Chippenham, Wilts

A CIP record for this book is available from the British Library

ISBN 0 7486 1329 3 (hardback)
ISBN 0 7486 1328 5 (paperback)

The right of Richard Hogg
to be identified as author of this work
has been asserted in accordance with
the Copyright, Designs and Patents Act 1988.

Contents

To readers

This textbook is designed for students for whom this is the first experience of the language of the earliest period of English, namely the period from the time of the invasions of Britain by the English in the fifth century until the time of the Norman Conquest or shortly thereafter. If it is undoubtedly true that the first sighting of the English of that time comes as a shock to most beginning students, there can be no doubt that an understanding of that language is essential for a proper appreciation of how English has evolved over time.

The approach taken here is somewhat different from that usually taken in introductory textbooks of Old English. Most such books offer a two-part solution, consisting, firstly, of a freestanding account of the grammar, and, secondly, a group of texts which the student is expected to read by reference to the relevant material in the grammar. The distinctive feature of this work is that I have attempted to present an integrated account, in which, for the most part, accounts of the linguistic history of Old English are immediately followed by relevant and exemplary texts. Given the scope of this work, this has meant that some traditional features have had to be omitted. For example, there are no complete texts, except in one special case, and of necessity the grammar sections are also not as full as those which some textbooks provide. On the other hand, alongside some features not usually present at this level, such as a discussion of dialectal material, the material presented here is intended to provide the amount of work which can sensibly be covered in one-term or one-semester courses of the kind common today.

I have deliberately omitted some features which are usually included; in particular there is at no point any extended discussion of phonology. There is no doubt that the student who wishes to take his or her study of Old English further will need, at that stage, to acquire a deeper knowledge of the phonological features of the language. But my own experiences suggest that too great an emphasis on phonology at a very early stage actually inhibits an understanding of other linguistic matters and even of the reading of original texts. Also, unlike in the other texts in this series, there are no discussions of the exercises. This would have been pointless given that for the most part these exercises consist only of passages for translation.

Throughout this work I have tried, wherever appropriate, to relate Old English structures to those of the present day. The principal motivation for this is to demonstrate how much of the language has remained stable over time, rather than merely to assist the reader in his or her understanding of Old English. I am also aware that this work will often be used by readers whose first language is other than English, and therefore I have tried to relate Old English structures to those of our nearest relatives.

I owe a debt of gratitude to a variety of people. My thanks go to Heinz Giegerich, not merely for inviting me to write this work, but also for his helpful comments on the work as it progressed. Olga Fischer read the whole manuscript and suggested many improvements with her usual tact and intelligence. Some years ago I tested a small part of this work out on my students, and I am grateful to them for their responses at that time, as well as to my colleague Chris McCully for his valuable remarks on that first attempt. My thanks also go to my fellow authors Jeremy Smith and Simon Horobin for sharing their work on Middle English with me. Sarah Edwards, at Edinburgh University Press, has been incredibly patient with an author at whom she must have despaired, and I am grateful for her patience. In completing this work I have also benefited from the support of the Leverhulme Trust and their award of a Senior Research Fellowship, and for that support I am most grateful.

Finally, my sons have also read through parts of this work with an undergraduate's eye, and for that, and much more, I dedicate this book to them.

1 Origins and sources

1.1 Introduction

When did English begin? The question is often asked, but the answer is surprisingly dull. The standard view is that English began when the Anglo-Saxons began to settle in Britain. Who, then, were the Anglo-Saxons? Where did they come from? And when did they come to Britain?

From the accounts of Roman historians, especially Tacitus, we know that **Germanic** tribes had spread over northern Europe by the time of Christ. Such tribes did not form any unified confederation. Rather, they seemed to have been organised on a small group basis. Before the fifth century, the spread of these tribes did not include any part of Britain. Until AD 410 most of Britain had been under Roman control, although the native inhabitants were Celts, speaking various forms of **Celtic**, which give us present-day Welsh, Irish, Gaelic and (in Brittany) Breton, as well as the now-dead languages Cornish and Manx. No doubt many Celts also spoke Latin, the language of the Roman Empire.

Until the fifth century, therefore, there were few Germanic speakers in Britain, and most of those were almost certainly either in the Roman army or camp followers. But with the departure of the Romans, the continental Germanic tribes saw in Britain a nearby land ripe for the picking. The eighth-century English historian Bede tells of how, in AD 449, Hengist and Horsa were invited by the Celtic king Vortigern to help him against his enemies, and how they proceeded to establish a base for themselves in Kent. Bede also says that these first settlers came from three Germanic tribes, the Angles, the Saxons and the Jutes. Bede's account, no matter how careful, cannot be an entirely accurate reflection of what happened three centuries earlier, a period for which there were no contemporary records and whose history was recorded orally and passed down from generation to generation.

The language these settlers spoke was called *Englisc* (= English) by them, but it could not have been very different from the languages

1

spoken by those they had left behind on the mainland of Europe. Of course, if you compare present-day English with German or Dutch or Frisian you will immediately notice many differences. But these were absent, or only minimally present during the Anglo-Saxon period. In the last 1,500 years English has grown less and less Germanic in character. It is important to stress that there is a continuous, if sometimes shaky, line of development between Old English and present-day English. There is more in common between the two than first meets the eye, and I shall try to demonstrate these common factors as often as possible.

1.2 Indo-European and Germanic

I have introduced the term Germanic but have not given an explanation of it. So what does it mean? First of all, I should say that it does not equate to German. German is indeed a Germanic language, but Germanic is the term used to describe a group of languages which share a particular set of characteristics unique to them. We shall shortly see some examples of this, but here we need only list the more important present-day languages which are of Germanic origin: English, Frisian, Dutch, German, Danish, Norwegian, Icelandic, Faroese, Swedish and, outside Europe, Afrikaans (which is most closely related to Dutch). I have arranged these languages in an order which, broadly speaking, and ignoring the special case of Afrikaans, shows their relative linguistic closeness to English.

But this is not the whole story. For, just as English, German and so on all owe their origins to Germanic, so Germanic itself belongs to a much larger **language family**. This family is known as **Indo-European**, and to it belong other groups as well as Germanic, including Indic, Greek, Romance, Slavic, Baltic, Celtic and other less well attested groups. The various groupings stretch geographically from the Indian sub-continent to Ireland. Note that this means that the other native languages of the British Isles, Welsh, Irish and Gaelic, are ultimately related to English, although only distantly.

It is probably very difficult to appreciate how similar the wide variety of Indo-European languages are. This is partly simply because the relations we are talking about stem from a period almost 10,000 years ago, and for which we have no direct evidence. The way we overcome this is by searching for what are called **cognate** forms. These are words which share meanings over different languages and which appear to have similar shapes. Thus, if we search for cognates in Sanskrit (an ancient language of India), Greek, Latin and English, we find the following words for 'father':

Sanskrit	Greek	Latin	English
pitā	patēr	pater	father

Notice that in the first three languages the first consonant is always **p** and the middle one **t**, and we can guess that the final -*r* was somehow lost in Sanskrit.

English looks different, especially in terms of the first consonant. But if we compare not only 'father' with 'pater', but also other English and Latin words, such as 'fee' and 'pecus', or 'first' and 'primus', 'foot' and 'pedem', you may be able to see that English **f** often corresponds to Latin **p**. This process, which is called **comparative reconstruction**, is fraught with dangers, but all I want to do here is to give you an idea of what is done.

It is also possible to use comparative reconstruction on more closely related languages, such as the Germanic group. Below I give some examples of cognate forms from English, Dutch and German, and alongside them I give the corresponding French words:

English	Dutch	German	French
father	vader	Vater	père
foot	voet	Fuss	pied
tooth	tand	Zahn	dent
ten	tien	zehn	dix

It will be clear that English and Dutch share much in common, and that German is not hugely different (although the initial consonant **t** has changed to **z**). Of course the reason for this is that all three are Germanic languages. French, on the other hand, is a Romance language, deriving from Latin. Therefore it is much more distantly related. Note that where English has **f** French has **p**, just like the words for 'father' above. You should also be able to work out that there is a further parallel relationship between **d** and English **t**.

1.3 The Anglo-Saxon settlement

It is likely that the Anglo-Saxons, or more properly, the English (see below), came from the area of north-west Germany and Denmark, and perhaps also the north-east of the Netherlands, the area known today as Friesland. Indeed Frisian, still spoken by about 300,000 people in this part of the Netherlands, is the language to which English is most closely related historically. Despite the story of Hengist and Horsa, when the English came to Britain they did not settle only in Kent. At much the same time they also settled along the east coast south of the Humber, especially in East Anglia. Soon after they spread westwards and northwards, and by the seventh century the English (as they called themselves = Old English *angelcynn*) had settled in almost all of England and southern Scotland, the main exceptions being Cornwall and parts of north-west England.

In other words, these new immigrants to Britain established themselves as the dominant group within two centuries. There is more than one reason why this could happen. It is possible that climatic changes led to population pressure on the continent, and certainly there were major movements in population throughout central Europe at the time. Since Germanic mercenaries had been in the Roman army the Germanic tribes would have heard about Britain from them as well as others. And the departure of the Romans seems, as Bede indicates, to have left a power vacuum, which the English were easily able to exploit.

1.4 The look of Old English

When studying Old English the first thing that has to be done is to look at its spelling system or **orthography**. The reason for this will be immediately apparent, for Old English orthography is rather different from that in PDE (present-day English). This is despite the fact that the Anglo-Saxons used basically the same alphabet as we do. The most obvious difference is that the Anglo-Saxons did not use the following letters: <j, v>, and the following were very rare: <k, q, x, z>. On the other hand, they had several letters which we use either very rarely or not at all: <æ, þ, ð>. In addition, some Old English letters had a range of usage different (sometimes very different) from that today. A list of Old English and PDE correspondences is given below:

Old English	PDE
æ	a
c	c, k, ch
f	f, v
g	g, y
s	s, z
þ, ð	th
y	i

In addition, there were several **digraphs**, that is, combinations of two letters to represent a single sound, just like PDE <th> does in 'thin'. The Old English digraphs and their PDE correspondences are listed below:

Old English	PDE
cg, gg	dg(e), gg
sc	sh, sk
hw	wh
hr, hl, hn	r, l, n

Of the correspondences, the ones which will give you most difficulty are <c> and <g>, which each have two very distinct values, even when they are part of a digraph. In order to help you distinguish the cases, I shall follow a very common editorial practice and place a dot over <c>, i.e. <ċ>, when it corresponds to PDE <ch>. Similarly, when <cg, sc> represent the equivalents of <dg(e), sh> respectively, I shall place the same dot over <g> and <c> when it corresponds to <dg(e), sh>, i.e. <ċġ, sċ>.

There can be no doubt that at first sight Old English orthography can be confusing. It certainly adds to the difficulties in studying an unfamiliar language. The differences, however, should not be exaggerated, and often these differences are quite transparent. Here are some examples of Old English words:

drifen   hætt   ġear   þæt   lytel   ðe

and here are their PDE equivalents:

driven   hat   year   that   little   the

One or two spelling conventions which I have not mentioned may cause initial difficulty. For example, the doubling of consonants in *hætt* and the reverse situation in PDE *little* is confusing. Nevertheless the basic patterns should be easily understood.

1.5 Vowels

When we look more closely at vowels, then we quickly come across more serious problems. Whereas today we regularly distinguish between long and short vowels, so that long vowels often (but not always!) have distinctive spellings, such as <ou, oo, oa, ee, ea>, in Old English there were no distinctions made between long and short vowels. Editors often distinguish between long and short vowels by placing a dash or **macron** over long vowels, so that we find *rīse* 'I rise' but *risen* 'risen'.

Even with long vowels, however, it is possible to give some guidelines. Thus, if the Old English spelling is <ā>, then respell it as either <oo> or <o> + consonant + <e>, and if the spelling is <ū> respell it as <ou>. Many of the other correspondences can be solved with a little ingenuity.

Take, for example, the following sentences:

> Hwī stande ġe hēr ælne dæġ æmtiġe?
> þa arās he from þæm slēpe
> Wæs he se man in woruldhāde ġeseted

If we try only to replace the Old English spellings with corresponding PDE ones, and don't attempt any translation, then those such as the following should result:

> Why stande ye here allne day amtiye
> Tha arose he from tham sleep
> Was he se man in woruldhood yesetted

It is true that for any beginner there are still a number of mysteries, but the number is significantly reduced, to the extent that a plausible attempt at translation may be possible.

It is important to emphasise what we have not done so far, as well as what we have done. I have avoided too specific a discussion of pronunciation, preferring to suggest some relatively straightforward way of respelling Old English to make the relationships between Old English and PDE more transparent. Broadly speaking, the pronunciation of English did not change drastically between Old English and Middle English. Therefore, if you know what Chaucer's pronunciation was like, this will be a good, if approximate, guide to how Old English was pronounced.

1.6 People, places and texts

I shall return to the question of pronunciation at the end of this chapter, but it is also necessary to fill in a few more details about Anglo-Saxon England. The consolidation of the settlement is symbolised by what we call the Heptarchy, or the seven kingdoms of Wessex, Essex, Sussex, Kent, East Anglia, Mercia and Northumbria. Whether the Heptarchy represents a reality or a fiction remains up for debate, but the location of these areas suggests that by far the heaviest concentration of settlement was in the south and the east.

Nevertheless, the most powerful area by about 700 was probably Northumbria, where the most important centres were Durham and York. Northumbria had as its arch rival the kingdom of Mercia, whose centre was Lichfield, about twenty miles north of Birmingham. During the next century Mercia gradually became dominant. However, after the first quarter of the ninth century the north and midlands became more and more under Viking attack and the principal southern kingdom,

Wessex, began to assume dominance as the only area capable of resisting these attacks. This was particularly true during the reign of Alfred (871–99), who signed the Treaty of Wedmore. This established peace with the Danes, who controlled the area known as the Danelaw.

One of the best pieces of evidence for the extent of Viking settlement comes from place-names. In areas where the Vikings settled they named places with their own names. These can still be identified today, for example by the use of the suffix -*by*, the Danish word for 'farm', and a fairly common Norwegian suffix is -*thwaite* 'a clearing'. Thus it would be very difficult to find a more south-westerly example of -*by* than *Rugby* in Warwickshire, and -*thwaite* is virtually restricted to Cumbria (Westmorland and Cumberland) and North Yorkshire (although there is an odd patch of this suffix in East Anglia).

The various patterns of settlement have an enormous influence on the distribution of the texts which survive from the Old English period. The vast majority of texts come from the southern part of England, especially from the upper Thames valley and around Winchester, the principal town of Wessex. Other major centres include Canterbury, Lichfield, Worcester and Durham. In every case we are talking about texts which are almost all written in ecclesiastical centres.

In this book, as is common in initial studies of Old English, our main focus will be on West Saxon texts, that is to say, on the texts which originate from around the Winchester area. It is customary to divide West Saxon texts into two major groups: Early West Saxon and Late West Saxon. The texts belonging to the first group were written round about the time of Alfred or just after. In this group there are three fundamental texts: *Pastoral Care*, a translation of a major Christian treatise; the *Anglo-Saxon Chronicles*, or , rather, the parts of the *Chronicles* associated with Alfred; and *Orosius*, again a translation (and rewriting) of a text written by a late Roman historian. For Late West Saxon the most important texts are those of Ælfric, a monk writing at the end of the tenth century. Although Ælfric was trained at Winchester, he probably came from further north in Wessex. He wrote a compilation of *Lives of Saints* and a great many homilies. Ælfric is particularly important because he obviously took great care in composition, style and language, so that the regularity of his language begins to approach the level of a **standard language**. There is not the degree of standardisation to which we are accustomed in the present day, but there can be no doubt that this was an important factor in the widespread use of West Saxon in many parts of the country.

Present-day textbooks always use West Saxon as their basis for the introduction of Old English, and indeed, given the relative paucity of text from elsewhere, there is no alternative. One important warning, however, must be offered. In the overall history of the language, West Saxon is of only small relevance. The areas which come to dominate, in particular, the standard language of England today arise principally from the areas of the dialects of the East Midlands and East Anglia, areas for which, unfortunately, there is precious little Old English evidence.

Another complication arises from the fact that the dialects of Early West Saxon and the dialects of Late West Saxon differ in some significant features. Textbook writers, therefore, have made a decision about which form of the language to use when, for example, they present the different forms of nouns, adjectives, pronouns and verbs. In this book I shall use Late West Saxon as the basis for discussion. I do this for several reasons. Firstly on the grounds of quantity: there is so much more, both of prose and of poetry, which is written in Late West Saxon. Secondly, because that material is more homogenous than any other body of material. This second point is particularly important for the beginning student, who may not before have encountered historical texts such as those in Old English. For one of the immediate issues that arises is that in such texts there can be a wide variation in the shape of individual forms, even from sentence to sentence, which can cause considerable confusion. At least for Late West Saxon such variation is minimised.

1.7 The sound system of Old English

We have already explored some of the similarities and the differences between Old English and PDE in terms of their spelling systems. However, there is no disguising the fact that, nevertheless, there have been many major changes in pronunciation since the Old English period (and indeed considerable variation between dialects during the period itself). Of necessity, the study of the sound system, or **phonology**, is technical, and an understanding of key concepts such as the **phoneme** is important, but outside the scope of this work (you should consult, for example, the companion volume on phonology in this series, which you will find in the section on recommended reading).

The consonants of Old English are often recognisably parallel to those of PDE. Thus there were three voiceless stops: /p, t, k/ but only two voiced ones: /b, d/. The missing voiced stop, /g/, is discussed immediately below. The fricative system was radically different, for there were only voiceless phonemes, and three of these: /f, θ, x/. This does not mean that there were no voiced fricative sounds, for there were. The critical feature is that voiced sounds were in what is called **complementary distribution** with the voiceless ones. That is to say, when a fricative phoneme occurred at the beginning or end of a word, then it was produced as voiceless, but in the middle of a word it was produced as voiced. Thus the word *full* 'full' would have been phonetically [full], and the word *drīfan* 'drive' would have been [driːvan]. But phonemically both fricatives would have been /f/, i.e. /full/, /driːfan/. The development of a contrast between voiceless and voiced fricatives, as in standard PDE *ferry* vs. *very*, is a feature of the Middle English period. Another feature about the fricatives is more obvious, namely the presence of /x/, which does not occur in PDE. This voiceless **velar** fricative is comparable to the same sound in German and Dutch *hoch*, *hoog* 'high' so we find OE *hēah*. If we stay with the word *hēah*, it is worth noting that the initial consonant, although originally [x], had changed into the glottal fricative [h] by the OE period, thus already having the pronunciation it has in PDE. However, phonemically it remained an **allophone** of the phoneme /x/, and as we shall see below, it contrasts with the initial sound of a word such as *guma* 'man'.

As with the other fricatives, the velar is voiced medially, but exceptionally this sound, [ɣ], appears to have been a separate phoneme /ɣ/. It occurs initially, as in *guma* 'man', and medially, as in *dagas* 'days'. But it does not appear finally, where the sound is voiceless, hence /x/, as in *sorh* 'sorrow'. This voiced fricative is difficult for PDE native speakers to produce, since it is foreign to the present-day sound system. Since it is known that by the very end of the period the initial sound was developing to /g/, it makes sense to substitute that phoneme when reading. Similarly, the medial sound was to develop later into a variety of other sounds, and it may ease your introduction into the OE sound system if you use /w/, especially when the etymology suggests that that is the later state of affairs, as in *boga* 'bow'.

There were two sibilant phonemes, /s/ and /ʃ/, but only the former had a voiced allophone medially. Otherwise they behave in a fashion parallel to the fricatives. I shall discuss the behaviour of /ʃ/ further below. In addition to these sibilants, OE also had two affricates, namely /tʃ/, as in *ċyriċe* 'church', and /dʒ/, as in *eċg* 'edge', see §1.4 for the spelling of the affricates.

Unlike the situation in PDE, there were only two nasal phonemes in OE, namely /m/ and /n/. The difference arises because in OE when the phonetic sound [ŋ] occurs, it is always followed by either [k], as in *panc* 'thank', or [g], as in *sing* 'sing'. Therefore it remains an allophone of /n/. In standard PDE, on the other hand, final [g] has been lost, so that /ŋ/ is phonemic. It is worth noting that in the English Midlands the situation is close to the OE one, for there the final [g] has remained.

As in PDE there were two phonemic liquids in OE, namely /l/ and

/r/. The former was similar to that in PDE, and probably had two allophones, 'clear' [l] initially and 'dark' [ł] elsewhere, as in *lytel* 'little', where in both OE and PDE the first *l* is clear and the second *l* is dark. The one thing about /r/ of which we can be certain is that its pronunciation was quite different from that of PDE /r/. It is probably impossible, at this distance, even to attempt accuracy. Perhaps a sound in the range between an alveolar trill and a flap would be most appropriate. Finally, and before final consonants, it may well have had a retroflex or velarised component. Whatever the case, it must be observed that a postvocalic /r/ is always pronounced, in contrast to the situation in PDE. Initial and final examples are *rīdan* 'ride' and *heard* 'hard'.

There are two further consonants to mention, namely the approximants /j/ and /w/. Neither is particularly difficult and they are both directly reflected in the corresponding PDE forms. Phonologically they are the consonantal counterparts of the high vowels /i/ and /u/. The real problems with both of them, and especially with /j/, lie in the complexity of the OE spelling system, but see §1.4 for some help in this area.

There are two areas where OE had distinctive characteristics which are no longer present in PDE. Firstly, we find initial clusters consisting of /x/ + liquid, nasal or approximant, i.e. /xl-, xr-, xn-, xw-/, as in *hlūd* 'loud', *hring* 'ring', *hnægan* 'neigh', *hwæt* 'what'. Although almost all of these clusters have been simplified in PDE, there is a clear remnant of /xw-/ in those, mainly Scots, dialects which distinguish between /w/ and /ʍ/, as in *weather* vs. *whether*. Note that the spelling <wh-> rather than the OE <hw-> is of ME origin, and due to **Anglo-Norman** influence. Secondly, OE possessed **geminate**, or long, consonants, which occurred in medial position. Thus we find examples such as *hoppian* 'hop' vs. *hopian* 'hope'. These geminates may seem strange, but the phenomenon is by no means confined to OE. See, for example, Italian, where there is a similar phenomenon, and long consonants appear frequently, as in *sorella* 'sister'. Note also that there is no variation in the pronunciation of the first vowel in each word, as there mostly is in present-day English. At one stage in the history of OE these geminates must have occurred in final position too, and this accounts for spelling variations such as both *bedd* and *bed* for 'bed'. It is this presence of geminates which accounts for the failure of /ʃ/ ever to be voiced, because a word such as *fiscas* 'fishes' had a medial geminate, and this prevented voicing.

There were seven long and seven short vowels in OE: three front, three back, and one front rounded vowel, to which I shall return. There is a major difference between OE and PDE, in that in the former vowel length is critical, whereas in PDE it is vowel quality which is critical. In

PDE, for example, the difference between the vowel of *feet* and that of *fit* is primarily determined by vowel quality, thus there is a contrast between /fit/ and /fɪt/. But in OE the contrast between, say, *bītan* 'bite' and *biter* 'bitter', is mainly of length, hence /biːtan/ vs. /bitər/. The three pairs of front vowels were: /iː/ ~ /i/, /eː/ ~ /e/, /æː/ ~ /æ/, and examples of the latter two pairs are: *mētan* 'meet' ~ *metan* 'measure'; *mǣst* 'most' ~ *mæst* 'mast'. It should now be obvious why I have always marked long vowels with a macron. The back vowels pattern in the same way. Therefore we find the following scheme: /uː/, *dūn* 'hill' ~ /u/, *dun* 'dun'; /oː/, *gōd* 'good' ~ /o/, *god* 'god'; /ɑː/, *bāra* 'hoary' ~ /ɑ/, *hara* 'hare'. It is at least arguable that the short vowels tended to be lower or more centralised than the long ones, so that, for example, short /e/ and /o/ were phonetically closer to [ɛ] and [ɔ] respectively, thus having a pronunciation quite close to that of *bed* and the Scottish pronunciation of *cot*. The systematic pairing of long and short vowels, although foreign to most dialects of PDE, is close to the systems operating in a language such as Modern German.

The final pair of vowels are the front rounded pair, /yː/ and /y/, as in *sȳll* 'pillar' and *syll* 'sill'. Although these are mostly absent from PDE, at least as far as standard varieties are concerned, they are quite easily equated to the German long and short umlauted ü in, say, *dünn* 'thin' or the same sound in French *lune* 'moon'.

In addition to these vowels, OE had four diphthongs, again paired off, so that we find <ēo> and <eo> as one pair, and <ēa> and <ea> as the other. Examples are *bēor* 'beer', *beofor* 'beaver' and *hēah* 'high', *heard* 'hard'. In dialects other than Late West Saxon, and occasionally even there, the diphthongs <īo> and <io> can also be found, but for our purposes these can be equated with <ēo>, <eo>. You may have noticed that I have not yet provided a proper phonological statement of these diphthongs. There is a reason for that. These diphthongs are amongst the most controversial issues in OE linguistics. This is not the place for a discussion of the controversy, but it is necessary to admit its existence. The critical issue is whether the so-called short diphthongs are indeed diphthongal, rather than monophthongal. Here I shall assume that the diphthongal interpretation is correct, partly because it seems more probable, partly because it is the simpler way to approach the question.

Under this assumption, the phonemic values for the diphthongs might appear to be approximately /eːo/ and so on. That might have been the case at one early stage, but it is certain that by the time of Ælfric the second element had been reduced to an unstressed element, which is called **schwa**. Thus we can give the following values to the first pair above: /eːə/, /eə/. The second pair, <ēa> and <ea>, do not have quite the shape you might expect, because it is agreed that the first element is a low vowel, not a mid one. Therefore we find /æːə/, /æə/.

You may come across another apparent pair of diphthongs, namely <īe> and <ie>. This pair can be found almost exclusively in Early West Saxon texts such as those associated with Alfred. In Late West Saxon they are replaced by one of the two monophthongs *i* and *y* under slightly complex conditions which we can ignore here.

Exercises

1. Using the discussion in §1.4, give the PDE equivalents of the following OE words:

ofer	mann	bedd	dæġ	sċip
fisċ	æsċ	þe	þorn	ðe
ðorn	hyll	þynn	cynn	miht

2. In §1.5 I gave some examples of some simplified OE sentences. Here are some further examples (again simplified). Try to turn them into PDE:

þā cwæð seo hāliġe Agnes ðus [seo = 'the']

Ðās martyras nǣron nǣfre on līfe þurh wīf besmtytene [the third and fourth words show a double negative construction!]

þā sume dæġ bæd hē þone bisċeop blætsian his ful [þone = 'the'; ful = 'cup']

3. Using an atlas find six place-names containing the suffix -*by* and three with the suffix -*thwaite*.

4. Alfred may have come from a place called Wilton; Ælfric from Abingdon; Bede from Jarrow and Offa ruled the Mercians at Lichfield. Find each of these places on a map.

5. Using an etymological dictionary, find one example of a word other than those in §1.7 which originally had the OE cluster /xn-/ and do the same for the other clusters noted in that section.

6. A further cluster which has been simplified in PDE is the cluster /wr-/. Find two words which once had that cluster and two other words with which they now share the same pronunciation, that is to say, they are **homophones**. Two other lost clusters are /gn-/ and /kn-/. Find two examples of each. Do not include loan-words such as *gnu*.

2 The basic elements

2.1 Change and continuity

As I made clear in Chapter 1, English is in origin a Germanic language. In the passage of time since the English arrived in Britain, these Germanic origins have to a remarkable degree been obscured in various ways. Thus, for example, about a third of English vocabulary is non-native. The most prominent source of non-native vocabulary is French, but even quite early on the language took words from other languages, notably from Latin and the Scandinavian languages, a point I touched upon in §1.6 in relation to place-names. However, if we restrict ourselves to Old English, then even Scandinavian words are very rare right up to the end of the period, and French words all but non-existent. As I discuss later in the book, Old English did have a substantial number of words taken from Latin, notably, but not exclusively, in the language of the church.

Although what I have just said is true, and it is indeed the case that a substantial proportion of even the quite basic vocabulary of present-day English post-dates the time of Norman Conquest, this is by no means the whole story. For just as there have been substantial changes in the vocabulary since that date, so too have there been substantial changes in every other aspect of the structure of the language. Let me exemplify this by one example each from phonology, morphology and syntax, more or less at random.

In phonology I mentioned in §1.7 that Old English had geminate consonants, giving the examples *hoppian* 'hop' and *hopian* 'hope'. Present-day English, however, has no such contrast. Staying with these examples, you should be able to see that both these verbs share an ending, namely *-ian*. This is an ending which demonstrates that these verbs have been quoted in their **infinitive** form. But in present-day English the infinitive form of verbs is uninflected. Indeed, one of the most obvious differences between Old English and present-day English is that the former is clearly a reasonably fully inflected language, much like present-day German. But present-day English has only a very few inflections, such as the plural and the possessive of nouns. There was much more variety in Old English. Finally, in syntax, we do not find constructions such as the present-day English 'I will arise', for in Old English such usage is expressed by the simple present tense (occasionally with the addition of an adverb such as *nu* 'now').

It is important to recognise that these differences between Old English and present-day English are not necessarily due to English having lost its essential Germanic structure (although there is a perfectly acceptable argument for claiming that is actually the case). These differences arise from many, often unrelated, sources. Their overall effect on the present-day reader, however, is indeed to disguise the genuine continuities which persist throughout all ages. Here I shall always strive to emphasise those continuities.

2.2 Nouns

If we take a basic simple sentence in Old English, such as:

(1) Se guma slōh þone wyrm
     The man slew the dragon

then it would appear as if word order in Old English was the same as in present-day English. Unfortunately that is far from generally true as we shall see later; however, it is a good place to start, since it postpones the need for immediate complication.

Now compare (1) with the following sentence:

(2) Se wyrm slōh þone guman
     The dragon slew the man

As in present-day English, swapping the subject and object of the sentence changes the meaning as well. Thus in (1) the subject of the sentence was *guma*, but in (2) the subject is *wyrm*, and *guman* is the object, just as in (1) *wyrm* was the object. Such examples are for the most part quite transparent and easy to recognise, except in two vital respects. Firstly, note that the *guma* of (1) is matched by the slightly different form *guman* in (2). Secondly, the Old English equivalent of 'the' has two quite different shapes: *se* and *þone*. Furthermore, the different shapes are associated not with the specific noun that follows it, but rather with, respectively, the subject and the object.

These two points are features which are associated with the inflectional properties of the language. Whereas in present-day English almost all nouns have an invariable shape except that an ending is added to distinguish plural from singular and also to show possession, in Old English nouns added rather more inflectional endings. Let me exemplify this with the noun *stān* 'stone':

	Singular	*Plural*
Nominative	stān	stānas
Accusative	stān	stānas
Genitive	stānes	stāna
Dative	stāne	stānum

Although everyone will be familiar with the concepts of **singular** and **plural**, only someone already familiar with a language such as German or Latin will be able to understand the remainder of what is going on here.

The table immediately above is traditionally referred to as a **paradigm**. A paradigm shows the variety of different forms which any given word can use according to certain principles which I shall explain shortly. But the most important point to bear in mind is that paradigms are an essential feature of Old English, although, equally, they are unnecessary paraphernalia in the description of present-day English (we could say that the paradigm of *stone* today was: *stone* ~ *stones* but that would just be useless clutter, not so in Old English).

Essentially, the paradigms of nouns contain information about three obligatory linguistic features: **number**, which needs no explanation here, **case** and **gender**. Both of these terms do have to be explained. Let me start with case. As we saw in (1) and (2) above, nouns may change their shape, i.e. they may acquire different endings, according to their function in any particular sentence. In examples (1) and (2), for example, although it may not yet be obvious, the subject of each sentence is in the nominative case, and the object in the accusative case. Indeed, a useful rule of thumb is that the nominative case equates to the subject, and the accusative case to the object.

You may, at this stage, wonder why cases are necessary. The simplest answer to this is to say they historically derived. The earlier languages from which Old English derived had such a case system, and naturally it was inherited by Old English. But that will not quite do. The really interesting question is whether or not case had a significant function. The answer to that is yes. Furthermore, it is intimately connected with the general structure of the language. For, alongside a sentence such (1), it was quite possible to find the type in (3), which, interestingly, can also be found in German:

(3) þone wyrm slōh se guma

Now the crucial point about (3) is that it has the same meaning as (1). More specifically, it does not have the meaning of (2). There is, to be sure, a somewhat different emphasis in (3) as opposed to (1): it doesn't really mean 'the man slew the dragon' but rather something like 'it was the dragon that the man slew'. Notice, of course, that both Old English and present-day English can express both shades of meaning. But whereas today we have to use quite complex syntactic structures, in Old English the availability of case inflexions allows a much freer word order than is possible today and gives flexibility that has now been lost. We make up for that, of course, in not having to worry about case inflexion. As is so often the case, it's swings and roundabouts.

The other two cases are more complex, unfortunately, but in the case of the genitive it does no harm to start off anachronistically and say that the genitive is very similar to the present-day possessive in its range of uses. This provides at least a core meaning which we can expand upon at later stages. The dative case is also complex in make-up but again it is possible to identify one particular meaning which can be related to a present-day usage and to which further meanings can be added at appropriate moments. This usage is the Old English equivalent to the present-day indirect object construction. Thus:

(4) Tell *your people* a more hateful tale

is simply a direct translation of the Old English sentence:

(5) Seġe *þinum lēodum* miċċle lāþre spell

where I have italicised the indirect object in (4) and the original dative object in (5).

Now examine the following paradigm for *sċip* 'ship':

	Singular	Plural
Nom.	sċip	sċipu
Acc.	sċip	sċipu
Gen.	sċipes	sċipa
Dat.	sċipe	sċipum

As you will see, it is almost identical to the paradigm for *stān*, the only differences being in the nominative and accusative plural. But why is there such a difference there? The answer comes with the third obligatory feature I mentioned above, namely gender. For whereas *stān* is a noun of masculine gender, *sċip* is neuter. Being neuter it has its own set of neuter endings, although admittedly they are only slightly different from the masculine endings.

Those of you who are familiar with a language such as German or French will have come across the concept of grammatical gender in those languages. But others of you may find the concept very new. Grammatical gender is found in many, but by no means all, of the world's languages. In the Germanic languages it is a longstanding historical feature, which has persisted everywhere except in English. Although its origins are complex, for our purposes it is best to assume that every noun belongs to one of three genders: masculine, neuter and feminine (I place them in that order deliberately and for reasons that will become clear shortly; it is not a piece of sexism!). Although there is sometimes a correspondence between grammatical and natural gender, there are too many examples of the opposite for that correspondence to be widely helpful. For example, three common words meaning 'woman' in Old English are: *wifmann*, *hlæfdige* and *wif.* The first is masculine, the second feminine, the third neuter.

You may have spotted earlier, in examples (1) and (2), that the word *guma* changed its shape, to *guman*, when it appeared in object position rather than as subject. That variation cannot, obviously, be contained in the paradigm associated with *stān*, in contrast to the case of *wyrm*. This brings in another concept, namely that of **declension**. If any particular noun has the same set of endings as any other noun, then we can say that the two nouns share the same paradigm. Thus *stān* and *wyrm* share the same paradigm. All nouns which share that paradigm are said to belong to a particular declension. We can give a name to this declension for ease of reference. Let us call it the **General Masculine declension**. Similarly, *scip* belongs to the **General Neuter declension**.

The problem with *guma* ~ *guman* arises because it belongs to another declension, which we can call the **N declension**. The reason it has this name will be obvious when you consider the paradigm:

	Singular	*Plural*
Nom.	guma	guman
Acc.	guman	guman
Gen.	guman	gumena
Dat.	guman	gumum

Unlike the other two declensions we have seen, this declension contains nouns of all three declensions, although there are few neuter nouns; the only ones you are likely to see are *ēare* 'ear' and *ēage* 'eye'. Note also that both feminines and neuters have -*e* in the nominative singular, and neuters also have -*e* in the accusative singular.

If you feel uncomfortable with declensions, it is worth noting that you could use the concept for present-day English too, although it is scarcely needed. But you could talk about the s-declension, which would contain the overwhelming majority of nouns; other, minor, declensions might contain either only one member, such as *ox*, or only a few, such as the one containing animal names such as *deer, sheep*.

I have not yet considered the **General Feminine declension** nouns. The reason for this is that they have a somewhat different shape, historically. Whereas it should be clear that the general masculine and neuter nouns are very closely related, this is not true of the feminines, as can be seen from the following paradigm for *talu* 'tale':

	Singular	*Plural*
Nom.	talu	tala
Acc.	tale	tala
Gen.	tale	tala
Dat.	tale	talum

This completes what we can call the major declensions of Old English. As I shall discuss later, there are a number of variants of these declensions. There are also some minor declensions, so called because although they contain many important words they are not productive, that is to say, new words entering the vocabulary fit into one of the four classes above, rather than into any of the minor declensions. Of the four declensions, the most frequent is the general masculine, with about thirty-five per cent of nouns, whilst the general neuters and feminines account for about twenty-five per cent each. In the N declension, which accounts for the remainder, there are more masculines than feminines.

2.3 Demonstratives

One point which you may have noticed in the discussion above is that case forms are often of little help in determining the function of a noun in a sentence, and this can be seen without even having inspected any real examples. It is observable from the fact that so many of the case forms above are identical, not only from declension to declension, but within declensions too. Look, for example, at how many forms of the N declension are identical or note that similarly identical forms can be found in the general feminine declension. Such facts play an important role in the eventual loss of declensions, and gender, in English. But in Old English the declensional system remains relatively intact. An interesting question, therefore, is why that should be. It cannot be due merely to the forces of inertia.

The answer is that the noun declension system was supported from elsewhere in the system, in particular by the demonstrative system. Even more specifically, the Old English demonstrative *se*, which functioned both as a demonstrative with the meaning 'that' and as the equivalent to present-day English 'the', played a crucial role. Furthermore, this demonstrative had a full range of case forms, except that there is no gender distinction in the plural. Here is the paradigm of the demonstrative:

	Masculine	*Neuter*	*Feminine*	*Plural*
Nom.	se	þæt	sēo	þā
Acc.	þone	þæt	þā	þā
Gen.	þæs	þæs	þǣre	þāra
Dat.	þǣm	þǣm	þǣre	þǣm

A couple of footnotes are necessary here. Firstly, although I have marked the length of the long vowels, this is variable, and they would shorten in unemphatic contexts, just like demonstratives today. Secondly, demonstratives have an additional case, which is called the **instrumental** case. It only shows itself in the masculine and neuter singular, having the shape *þȳ*. Elsewhere in the paradigm the dative form is used instead. The instrumental is of mixed origin, but it suffices to say that in Old English it is thoroughly confused with the dative which tends to replace it.

The most important point, however, remains the fact if what we may, with some licence, call the definite article, is associated with a noun, then the degree of uncertainty caused by the presence of a noun standing alone is perceptibly diminished. This is true not only when the article is present, but also when its counterpart *þes* 'this' is present, for it too is fully inflected for case, number and gender. *þes* is much more like present-day 'this' than *se* is like 'that', in that it acts almost always with reference to a nearby event whereas *se* most often refers to a specified item. In present-day English we have three terms: namely the specific *the* and then two contrasting words showing either nearness (*this*) or distance (*that*). This latter contrast is usually referred to as **deixis**, and it should be clear that the same opposition is not so clear-cut in Old English.

2.4 Pronouns

The set of personal pronouns in Old English was more extensive than the one that we have today, but nevertheless the paradigms are easily understood. There are occasional ambiguities, but these are quite isolated and therefore you should quickly come to know where such problems arise. In presenting the personal pronoun paradigms I shall deal firstly with the first and second person pronouns, before discussing the third person ones.

The paradigm of the first person pronouns is as follows:

	Singular	Plural
Nom.	iċ	wē
Acc./Dat.	mē	ūs
Gen.	mīn	ūre

There are a few points to note. First of all, there is no distinction between accusative and dative forms. This is also true in the second person (but not the third person). For those of you familiar with German, which has accusative *mich* and dative *mir*, this is an obvious difference. The simplification in English is the result of the loss of certain final consonants, and it is the result of mere chance, rather than a deliberate structural change. Indeed, there are a few early texts which do have distinctive accusative forms. Secondly, there is a further set of pronouns which reflect an older number system, where there were distinctive forms for reference to two people. This is called the **dual** number, and the forms are: Nom. *wit*, Acc./Dat. *unc*, Gen. *uncer*. The dual is not always used, and when it is used it is often to make clear that the reference is to two people only. Thirdly, it should be noted that the first and second person genitive forms have an adjectival function, and this means that when they function as adjectives they take the appropriate adjectival inflection (see Chapter 3). Finally it should be noted that, as with the demonstratives, long vowels were often unstressed and shortened in context.

The second person pronouns are as follows:

	Singular	Plural
Nom.	þū	ġē
Acc./Dat.	þē	ēow
Gen.	þīn	ēower

The same remarks as for the first person pronouns apply here, and so, for example, there is a parallel dual paradigm, with the three forms *ġit, inc, incer*. But the most important point here is that there were separate singular and plural forms. Furthermore, the singular and plural forms do not operate as in, say, French, where *tu* is only used in familiar and colloquial contexts. In Old English the singular forms are always singular and the plural forms always plural, without exception. The development of the use of the plural in singular contexts started only in the Middle English period. You may also be able to spot that present-day English *you* is related to the Old English accusative plural rather than the nominative plural (which gives *ye*). This development is later still.

It is likely that the Middle English use of the plural in singular contexts arose firstly in formal contexts, although in relatively recent English it is the use of *thou* rather than *you* which has become a sign of formality, as in religious language. Of course in some dialects, for example in Yorkshire, the distinction between singular and plural can remain. On the other hand, some dialects have evolved a new plural form, such as *youse* in Scots or *y'all* in the southern USA.

Let us now turn our attention to the third person pronouns. As today, there are three singular pronouns but only a single paradigm for the plural. In Old English the singular pronouns correspond to the three grammatical genders, whereas in present-day English we use natural gender in almost all instances. In Old English there still remained a preference for grammatical gender everywhere, except that there was a strong tendency to use natural gender when referring back to humans, as in:

(6) And [God] ġeworhte of ðām ribbe ænne [MASC] wifman, and axode Adam hū hēo [FEM] hatan sċeolde

And God created from the rib a woman, and asked Adam what she should be called

But there is, nevertheless, a clear distinction between the Old English and present-day usages, although sentences such as (6) may be the first signs of the coming change.

As we mentioned above, there are separate accusative and dative forms. The forms are as follows:

	Masculine	Neuter	Feminine	Plural
Nom.	hē	hit	hēo	hī
Acc.	hine	hit	hī	hī
Gen.	his	hit	hire	hira
Dat.	him	him	hire	him

There are several points to note here. Perhaps the first of these concerns the plural forms, which all have an initial <h>. You must be careful to distinguish these forms from the present-day English ones which all start with <th>. The two are quite different. The ones we have today are due to influence from Scandinavian which begins after the Old English period and only appears throughout the country towards the very end of the Middle English period. If you look again at the forms above you will be able to see that in Old English every third person pronoun begins with <h>, and all these are the historically expected forms. Another form which is very different from that found today is *hēo* as against *she*. Again the changes occur during the Middle English period, so that all we do is note the later change.

It is impossible to ignore the fact that this third person system can be confusing when confronted with actual text, even though the paradigm above looks quite simple. You may already have noted two potential difficulties, namely that the feminine accusative and the plural accusative are identical, and that the same holds for the masculine/neuter dative and the plural dative. In fact the former pair are not too much of a problem, especially as there may be clues elsewhere, especially from the verb, but the latter can prove particularly difficult, even at a quite advanced stage.

The difficulties are further exacerbated by another feature which can be confusing for the modern reader. Although the forms given in the paradigm above are those most often used in Ælfric's writing, there is considerable variation in the forms used in other Old English texts, and indeed in Ælfric's own texts. Thus <i> is often replaced by <y>, e.g. *hym* etc. rather than *him*, and there are other variants too, e.g. *hiene* for *hine*, mostly in earlier texts associated with Alfred, or *heora* and *heom* for *hira* and *him*. The modern reader, who is used to a set spelling system, is tempted to see, for example, *heom* as a word quite distinct from *him* and it can be difficult to believe they are mere variants of one another.

But such variation is not the result of error. Recall my comments on standard language in Chapter 1. As I said there, even a writer such as Ælfric, who took great care over the forms of his language, was not writing in a standard language. Such a type of language requires an educational and political infrastructure of a degree which, despite the undoubted sophistication of the literate Anglo-Saxon community, was simply impossible. It is reasonable to talk of a **focussed** language, that is to say, a range of variation of linguistic forms which a geographically defined literate community shared to a considerable degree, but without themselves imposing a well-defined set of spelling conventions, or by using some external source such as a national educational policy. That idea, which may seem appealing today, would be a mere anachronism in the Old English context.

2.5 A simple sentence

We have now seen some of the more important elements of the noun phrase system of Old English, although obviously much is still missing (for example, we have said nothing about adjectives). At this stage it becomes possible to begin an analysis of some simple sentences which are genuine examples from Old English, that is to say, not, as before, examples wrenched out of context or adapted for purposes of exemplification. As you progress through this book you will discover that you will mostly have to work out the meaning of the texts yourself, with the aid of the glossary at the end. At the moment, however, that is clearly impossible, so every piece I use will be accompanied by a word-by-word translation. This, I have found, is one of the quickest and easiest ways of beginning to acquire some self-confidence in handling the language.

The first sentence which I have chosen comes from one of Ælfric's volumes of *Lives of Saints*. In Chapter 1 I wrote a little bit about Ælfric. During his lifetime Ælfric wrote a great many homilies and other sermons, as well as other works, including a Latin grammar to help the pupils in his monastery. There is good reason to start with Ælfric, for he writes with fluency and clarity and his work is amongst the easiest to understand. The short passage which I have chosen comes from his story of the Maccabees.

[₁Iūdas ðā ġelæhte þæs appollonies swurd,] [₂þæt wæs mærliċ wæpn,]
Judas then seized the Appolonius' sword,   that was famous weapon
[₃and he wann mid þam] [₄on ælċum gefeohte] [₅on eallum his līf.]
and he won with that   in each battle   in all his life

I have marked each major part of the sentence, concentrating on the noun phrases, so that we don't get confused by taking the complete sentence at one fell swoop.

In the first part the only phrase that is of major interest is *þæs appollonies swurd*. Note in particular that the demonstrative *þæs* is in the genitive because it agrees with *appollonies* in case, number and gender. It is interesting that this latter noun, a Latin proper name (as the gloss shows), is given an Old English inflexion. I hope also that you were able to observe the variation between <ð> and <þ> which was discussed in Chapter 1.

In the second clause, you probably expected an indefinite article, giving the equivalent of 'a famous weapon'. However, although Old English had the word *ān* 'one', this is not the exact equivalent of the present-day article, and when it is used in an article-like position it usually has a meaning closer to 'a certain'. In the clause above we have good confirmation that an article is not obligatory as it is today.

Moving now to the third part, the subject pronoun *he* followed immediately by the verb is exactly the same pattern as in the present-day language. The phrase *mid þam* will cause more difficulty. Here we have another example of variation, because it is another spelling of *þæm*, which is, of course, part of the demonstrative paradigm. Here the demonstrative is being used as a pronoun (as is equally possible in present-day English). It is in the dative case, unambiguously, and that is because it is governed by the preposition *mid*, but is it singular or plural?

It is singular, because it refers back to *swurd*. The phrase therefore means 'with that (sword)'. The fourth part of the sentence consists of a further phrase consisting of a preposition followed by a dative singular phrase, and exactly the same is true of the fifth and final phrase.

Finally in this chapter, let me take one further sentence from the same text, only a few lines below it. It should be noted that I have altered the form of one word in the text by changing its form to a more common (and less complex) variation. This time I have also omitted one or two of the present-day glosses:

Æfter ðysse sprǣċe hi ēodon togædere
_____ this speech they went _____
and Iūdas ða aflīgde þone fore-sǣdan Seron
__ ___ then defeated the aforesaid Seron

You should have had no difficulty in filling in the missing words, which follow the correspondences between Old English and present-day spellings discussed in Chapter 1.

The first difficulty here is the phrase *ðysse sprǣċe*. What is its case and gender? The governing preposition *æfter*, as I shall discuss later, usually takes the dative case. Is there any evidence to support this here? There are two different approaches. If we take the noun itself, its meaning tells us that it must be singular, and the ending -*e* is one we have only seen used in the dative singular. If we examine the demonstrative *ðysse*, then we can tell from what I have said above that the ending -*e* can only be feminine singular, for the masculine and neuter dative singular ends in -*um*. So we can be certain that the noun is a feminine noun. By now the paradigms of the personal pronouns and the definite article will be familiar, and therefore neither the pronoun *hi* nor the masculine accusative form *þone* will cause any problems. The remainder of the sentence will be transparent, given that I have glossed the verb forms, which we have not yet discussed.

In the next chapter I shall discuss some further details of noun inflection and also go on to discuss the inflectional forms of adjectives. The fact that adjectives can inflect may not seem surprising, but they have a rather unexpected feature in this context which you are unlikely to have come across unless you have a good knowledge of German. Adjectives, therefore, will warrant some serious attention.

Exercises

1. The following examples are inflectional forms from some of the paradigms given in this chapter. For each one give details exactly what form

of the word (i.e. case, number and gender) is being used. If the form is ambiguous, give both or all of the possible answers: (a) *naman* 'name'; (b) *hlāfas* 'loaf'; (c) *limu* 'limb'; (d) *sēo*; (e) *þē*; (f) *ðāra*. Note that here and below I give the singular of the present-day word. You will not always be able to determine the gender of some of these examples, but where you cannot do so, you should indicate the range of possibilities.

2. The following examples require the same type of answer as in (1), but this time the appropriate form of the definite article is also supplied: (a) *þā gyfa* 'gift'; (b) *þā hearpan* 'harp'; (c) *þāre fare* 'journey'; (d) *þaes landes* 'land'.

3. Exercises such as those in (1) and (2) are a good starting point, but there is no substitute for the task of actually understanding 'real' text. Following on, therefore, from the sentences we examined in this chapter, now attempt as full an analysis as possible of the extract from the same text which follows below. I have added glosses for items which you have not yet encountered and which are not immediately transparent:

Iūdas ðā befran his ġeferan rædes	asked; comrades' advice
and cwæð to Simone his ġesċeadwisan breþer	said; discreet; brother
ġecēos ðe nu fultum and far to Galilea	choose; assistance; go
and ġehelp ðīnum māgum ðe ðā manfullan besittað	kinsmen who the wicked harass
iċ and Ionathas mīn ġingra brōðor	younger
farað to Galáád to afflġenne þā hæðenan	defeat; heathens

3 More nouns and adjectives

3.1 Irregular nouns

The way in which I presented the noun inflections in Chapter 2 has two major defects. It did not account for a number of important exceptions to the paradigms (and on which I therefore was silent) and there was no attempt to present an overall view. These defects were inevitable at that stage, but it is now time to remedy them. My principal aim here will be to show that the nominal system of Old English was, for the most part, rational and simple. Of course, as with any real language, there were blips in the system, but these can be most easily understood in the context of the overall pattern.

The best starting-point is again the paradigm of *stān*, that is to say the paradigm of the general masculine nouns. I re-present that immediately below, but you will see that I have altered the presentation in one significant respect:

	Singular	*Plural*
Nom.	stān-Ø	stān-as
Acc.	stān-Ø	stān-as
Gen.	stān-es	stān-a
Dat.	stān-e	stān-um

The alteration consists in my having split each form into two parts, a **stem** and an inflection. The stem is the part of the word which contains the meaning associated with the lexical item, and the inflection carries the morphological and syntactic information (i.e. the case, number and gender). Both the stem and the inflection are called **morphemes**; the stem is said to be a **free** morpheme, because it has independent lexical status, whilst the inflection, which is dependent upon the existence of another morpheme to which it can be attached, is said to be **bound**. It may seem surprising that I have added what is called a **zero** morpheme, that is a morpheme which contains no phonetic material, to the nominative-accusative. We wouldn't normally do that for present-day English, because the language has changed its structure over time.

One advantage of this paradigm approach is that we can see clearly what it means to say that a noun belongs to this declension. It is the fact that all nouns of this declension, and only nouns of this declension, share exactly the same set of inflections. There is quite a lot resting on this claim, as we shall see. For example, there is a fair number of nouns which follow the pattern of *stān* in every respect except that they have a final *-e* in the nominative-accusative singular, e.g. *cyme* 'arrival'. Historically these nouns originate from an different declension which still existed at the earliest stages of the language. Rather than maintaining that this other declension survived, which could only be claimed at the expense of massive complication, what we do is suggest that this *-e* was part of the stem, and it was deleted before any following vowel. Thus the genitive singular form *cyme* would actually result from the structure *cyme+es* with deletion of the final *-e* of the stem.

A further sub-group, best represented by *here* 'army', shows a wide range of forms, for example *here, here, heriges* ~ *herġes* ~ *heres, heriġe* ~ *herġe here* and plural forms such as *heriġeas* ~ *herġeas* ~ *heras* and others. Originally, here too, such a noun belonged to another declension, but what we can witness as the language changes is the growing tendency of such a noun to follow the general masculine declension and to lose the older forms. So both the examples we have just discussed demonstrate simplification of the declensional system.

Let us now turn our attention to the General Neuter declension. As can be seen from the evidence in Chapter 2, this declension is only marginally distinct from the general masculines. Not surprisingly, therefore, it too has some nouns with a stem-final *-e* and such nouns follow, where there are no distinctions between the two declensions, exactly the same pattern as nouns such as *cyme*; a typical example would be *wīte* 'punishment'.

But in the case of the neuters I have so far ignored another important issue. For the paradigm I presented in Chapter 2, although it is correct, does not tell the whole story. Alongside a noun such as *scip*, we also find nouns such as *word* 'word' and *bān* 'bone'. For the most part they decline in the same way as *scip*, except that they have a different nominative-accusative plural. In these cases such nouns have shapes identical to the corresponding singulars, that is to say, the nominative-accusative singular of *word* is *word* and so too is the nominative-accusative plural; exactly the same parallel holds in the case of *bān*.

Of the two points that arise in this context, let me deal with the trickier one first. How can this type be held to be members of the general neuters? The answer to this is that it is possible to work out that these nouns must have at one time had a final *-u* just like *scip* but that there was an historical change by which final -*u* was dropped after a heavy syllable, that is to say, after either a long vowel and a consonant or a short vowel and two consonants. So at an early stage in the history this must have been no more than a normal sound change; but later, certainly before the time of Ælfric, the sound change had become an inflectional property, i.e. a morphological feature. We can tell that this is the case because final -*u* was retained in the verbal paradigm even although it was lost everywhere else, both in nouns and adjectives.

There are two other important points to be made here. Firstly, what you will have noticed is that the result of the change, as I have said, is to make the nominative-accusative singular and the nominative-accusative of these neuters identical. Now given that the distinction between singular and plural is one of the very few persisting and vital distinctions in English noun morphology, you would expect – indeed you know – that such neuter nouns would switch to having to the clearer ending -*as*. This, of course, is how they end up: present-day *bones*, *words*. But it should be noted that this development only takes place after the Old English period, for until then the grammatical gender system is strong enough to withstand an otherwise tempting change.

The second point refers back to the morphological status of this vowel loss, for it is not only neuters that are affected by the loss. Recall the feminine noun *talu*, which we used in Chapter 2 for the paradigm of general feminines. As you can see, this noun has a final -*u* in the nominative singular and its stem syllable is short. Therefore we should expect that there would be corresponding heavy-stemmed nouns without -*u*. That is indeed what happens, so that we find nouns such as *glōf* 'glove' and *ecg* 'edge'.

There are quite a number of other departures from the declensions given in Chapter 2. For the most part we don't have to worry ourselves with these at this stage, but I shall mention two of them which are quite common and therefore worth knowing immediately. The first of these concerns masculine and neuter nouns with the stem vowel *æ*, as in *dæg* 'day' and *fæt* 'vessel, vat'. In the plural of these nouns we find, instead of *æ*, the vowel *a*, thus *dagas* 'days', *fatu* 'vessels'. There is therefore a consistent contrast between the singular and plural forms which goes right through the paradigm. The second case is a matter of inflection in the general feminine declension, for there, and particularly with short-stemmed nouns, the genitive plural is often -*ena* rather than -*a*, e.g. *talena* rather than *tala*. I mention this simply because it can be confusing, since it can lead to the belief that the noun belongs not to the general feminines but to the N declension.

3.2 Minor declensions

I made a distinction earlier on between irregular declensions and minor declensions. Essentially that difference is between, on the one hand, unexpected variations within one of the standard paradigms, and, on the other hand, paradigms which, although they are internally regular and self-contained are nevertheless not productive in the Old English period.

In order to better understand what characterises a minor declension, I want to start this part of the discussion by looking at a minor declension which is not only important in Old English, but actually remains in present-day English. The most frequent example today is *man*, but of course we can add to that *foot, goose, louse, mouse, tooth* and *woman*. The distinguishing feature of them all is that they show a different vowel in the plural from that in the singular. In fact this doesn't quite fit as an expression of the alternation in *woman* ~ *women*, but here the spelling might help you to see that originally this word was a **compound** of the two Old English words *wīf* 'woman' and *man* 'person' (there was once also another, corresponding, compound *carl* 'man' plus *man*).

In Old English equally, all the above nouns belonged to this same declension, but there a few further members, most notably *āc* (fem.) 'oak', *bōc* (fem.) 'book', *burg* (fem.) 'castle', *cū* (fem.) 'cow', *fēond* (masc.) 'foe', *frēond* (masc.) 'friend' and *hnutu* (fem.) 'nut'. Of the nouns which survive today, *fōt, man, tōð* and *wīfman* were masculine in Old English, *gōs, lūs* and *mūs* feminine. There were never any neuter nouns in this declension. There are some minor variations between the masculine and feminine paradigms, but we need only present a single paradigm with the alternative feminine form in the genitive singular noted in brackets:

	Singular	*Plural*
Nom.	fōt	fēt
Acc.	fōt	fēt
Gen.	fōtes (bōċe)	fōta
Dat.	fēt	fōtum

The most obvious and the most important point to note is that the variation in stem vowel does not, as in present-day English, correlate directly with singular vs. plural. Instead, the vowel variation occurs in the dative singular and the nominative-accusative plural. Sometimes it is also found in genitive singular of feminines, so that we can find *bēċ* alongside *bōċe*. This variation was due to an earlier sound change which caused a vowel to be fronted when there was an i in the next syllable. Subsequently that i was lost, which makes the process, normally known as

umlaut or mutation, rather obscure. This declension, therefore, is usually known, both in Old English and today, as the **mutation declension**. I realise that at this point I have not properly explained the process of umlaut. However, I shall return to the issue in more detail in Chapter 4.

The mutation declension tells us quite a lot about the historical development of the language, for we can learn two opposing principles from that development. The first of these is that when a paradigm becomes obscured, most often because of phonological changes, then the members of the paradigm tend to attach themselves instead to another, more regular, paradigm. We can see that this has happened in, for example, the case of Old English *bōc* compared with present-day *book*. On the hand, the second principle states that if a word is very frequent, as in, say, *fōt*, then perceived irregularities may be preserved because of high frequency. The first principle can be seen at work in Old English. Thus some of the mutation nouns begin already in the Old English period to acquire the inflexions of a regular declension, so that we find *fēondas*, *frēondas* for earlier *fȳnd, frȳnd*. The second principle, of course, can only operate over a long period of time and is only seen in terms of preservation, that is to say it can only be confirmed by the fact that, for example, present-day *man* has kept the mutation vowel alternation.

There were three further minor declensions which are important because they each include some nouns which belong to core vocabulary, rather like those in the mutation declension. This is most obvious of all in what we may term the **kinship declension**. This declension consists of the four nouns *mōdor* 'mother', *brōðor* 'brother', *dohtor* 'daughter' and *sweostor*. These nouns are, to an even greater extent than the mutation declension, subject to considerable variation, but the following paradigm is perhaps the most usual:

	Singular	Plural
Nom.	mōdor	mōdru, mōdra
Acc.	mōdor	mōdor, mōdra
Gen.	mōdor	mōdra
Dat.	mēder	mōdrum

Sometimes in all of these nouns the nominative-accusative plural shows a zero inflection, e.g. *mōdor* 'mothers'. Exceptionally *sweostor* always has that uninflected form in the dative plural, but it will be clear that the other kinship nouns have, like the nouns of the mutation declension, an umlauted form there. The other word which might be expected to follow the kinship declension is, of course, *fæder* 'father'. In the singular this word does indeed usually follow the above paradigm, except that it is almost always not umlauted in the dative, and thus is uninflected throughout the singular. In the plural, however, at an early stage it appears to have shifted to the general masculine declension, so that its nominative-accusative plural becomes *fæd(e)ras*.

The second declension which must be mentioned is the *a*-**plural declension**. The paradigm of the word *sunu* 'son' is representative:

	Singular	Plural
Nom.	sunu	suna
Acc.	sunu	suna
Gen.	suna	suna
Dat.	suna	sunum

Another masculine example is *wudu* 'wood', whilst *duru* 'door' and *nosu* 'nose' are feminine. In addition the feminine noun *hand* 'hand', which also belongs to the *as*-plurals, has the same paradigm as above except that the nominative-accusative singular has no final *-u*. Perhaps you have worked out for yourself that this lack of final *-u* here has the same cause as the lack of final *-u* we have already seen in, for example, *word*. There are a few other words which originally belonged to the same declension, but in general these all follow the general masculine or general feminine declension according to their gender. This, of course, is quite a natural development, given my earlier comments.

Beyond these two minor declensions there are further nouns which originate from other older declensions. Thus although the neuter nouns *æġ* 'egg', *ċealf* 'calf', *ċild* 'child' and *lamb* 'lamb' appear by their singular forms to be normal general neuter nouns, in the plural they show *r* after their stem, so that we find, for example, *ċildru, ċildru, ċildra, ċildrum* although again, naturally, they sometimes align fully with the general neuter declension. Another, rather more numerous, group, which is related to the present participle *-end*, is composed of masculine agentive nouns such as *rīdend* 'rider'. They also appear in their singular forms to be identical to the general masculine declension. However, the usual plural forms at the time of Ælfric are: *rīdendras, rīdendras, rīdendra, rīdendum*, thus rather like *ċildru*. At an earlier stage it was more common to find *rīdend, rīdend, rīdenra, rīdendum*, but the extension of *-r-* elsewhere perhaps here, and more certainly still in the case of *ċildru*, seems to prefigure the later form *children*, also seen in *brethren*. It is sometimes claimed that *children* has a 'double inflection', with *-r-* followed by *-en*, but this may not be the best analysis, given that the *-r-* in *brethren* does not have an inflectional source, at least in terms of Old English.

The third minor declension is associated with the names of peoples and tribes. These words only appear in the plural, and therefore we can talk about the **plural declension**. The paradigm can be exemplified by *Engle* 'the English':

	Plural
Nom.	Engle
Acc.	Engle
Gen.	Engla
Dat.	Englum

Typical other examples include: *Dene* 'Danes', *Myrċe* 'Mercians', *Seaxe* 'Saxons', as well as the collectives *lēode* 'people', *ylde* 'men' and *ylfe* 'elves'. There is some variation in forms of the genitive, most notably in *Myrċna*, *Seaxna*. Early in the period there were rather more nouns in this declension; note particularly that the declension originally contained words with a full singular and plural paradigm. Perhaps the most frequent of these 'ordinary' words was *wine* 'friend' with plural *wine*. But these words adopt the paradigm of the general masculines, so that we find plurals such as *winas* 'friends'.

Why should this have occurred? Is it merely a symptom of the general tendency towards simplification in the set of paradigms? That can hardly be the case, because, after all, there is no reduction in the total number of different declensions. There seems to be a better motivation available. If *wine* had remained as it was earlier, then it would have continued to have identical nominative and accusative singular and plural forms. Even if it is true that we have seen other words where the same happens, for example in *word*, such a situation in a language for which the singular ~ plural contrast is important is clearly undesirable. Especially when, as here, there was an easy remedy, namely to shift a word such as *wine* to a different declension. Evidence that this is exactly what happened comes precisely from the nouns which were only plural: they did not shift declension, for they did not have a singular ~ plural contrast.

3.3 Adjectives

There are a few other scattered noun forms, but they are rather varied and also tend to assimilate to an appropriate more general declension so that we need not spend further time on them. Instead I want now to consider adjectives. Like the nouns, adjectives were inflected in Old English, and in doing so they agreed in case, number and gender with the noun they modified, just as they do in present-day languages such as French and German.

However, there is a major difference between adjective declension in, say, French on the one hand and Old English on the other. In this respect the behaviour in Old English is similar to that of present-day German. But for anyone unused to a system such as the latter, what happens in Old English will undoubtedly seem strange. For in both German and Old English the situation is that each adjective may follow two declensions and the declension to which an adjective conforms is determined by syntactic features.

What happens is as follows. Adjectives in Old English, as in present-day language, may be preceded by a demonstrative, such as *se* or *þes*, or a possessive, such as *mīn*, or a possessive noun or noun group. Taken together, these contexts may be defined as **definite** contexts. Of course, adjectives do not need to have a defining definite context. This is most obviously, but not only, the case when they follow a verb, as in present-day English *John is happy*. We can describe any such context as an **indefinite** context.

This contrast between definite and indefinite contexts is at the core of Old English adjective inflection. The fundamental decision in every case is whether the adjective is definite or indefinite. This determines which set of inflections, i.e. which declension, is used. Thus *the happy man* is in Old English:

(1) se glæd guma

whereas *a happy man* is:

(2) glæda guma

Thus adjective declensions are quite different from noun ones. Firstly, all adjectives – apart from a few special cases, which are mostly explicable on syntactic grounds – decline according to both the definite declension and the indefinite declension, as shown in (1) and (2) above.

Of the two declensions, the simpler is the definite declension, which closely follows the N declension discussed in Chapter 2, the principal difference being in the genitive plural, where there is, as we have seen elsewhere, an *-r-* immediately after the stem. Note also that there are no gender distinctions in the plural. I use the adjective *blinda* for exemplification:

	Masculine	*Neuter*	*Feminine*	*Plural*
Nom.	blinda	blinde	blinde	blindan
Acc.	blindan	blinde	blindan	blindan
Gen.	blindan	blindan	blindan	blindra
Dat.	blindan	blindan	blindan	blindum

Sometimes the genitive plural shows the inflection *-ena*, e.g. *blindena*.

The definite declension's closeness to the N declension makes it quite easy to follow, but the task is harder for the indefinite declension. There are two reasons for this. Firstly, as might be expected, just as the definite declension follows the N declension, so the indefinite declension follows the three general declensions. Therefore, there are rather more different declensional endings to cope with. Secondly, there is a further complication in that the endings used in the definite declension are sometimes quite different from those used in their apparent nominal counterparts. Furthermore, since each of the three nominal declensions has its own endings in the plural as well as the singular, so the indefinite adjective declension shows gender distinctions not only in the singular but also in the plural. The overall result is as follows, again using *blind* (note, by the way, that just as I used the nominative masculine singular form *blinda* as the citation form for the definite declension, now I use the corresponding indefinite citation form):

Singular	*Masculine*	*Neuter*	*Feminine*
Nom.	blind	blind	blind
Acc.	blindne	blind	blinde
Gen.	blindes	blindes	blindre
Dat.	blindum	blindum	blindre
Instr.	blinde	blinde	blindre
Plural			
Nom.	blinde	blind	blinda
Acc.	blinde	blind	blinda
Gen.	blindra	blindra	blindra
Dat.	blindum	blindum	blindum

It may be obvious that we have to make a series of remarks about this paradigm, for it inadequately represents the full state of affairs as it stands. Most obviously, you will have noticed that in the masculine and neuter singular, and only there, we find a separate instrumental inflection, as was seen in the demonstrative. The other point which we should note immediately is what happens if the adjective is short-stemmed, rather than long-stemmed as is the case with *blind*. The long-stemmed adjectives are, despite some differences, fundamentally allied to the corresponding general declensions. Therefore, just as the feminine noun *talu* (see Chapter 2), has a final *-u* in the nominative because it is short-stemmed, so too should a short-stemmed adjective have final *-u*. And that is what we find. Thus *trum* 'firm' has nominative singular *trumu*. And similarly, of course, in the nominative-accusative plural of the neuter, we also find *trumu*.

There are other issues too, for example the variation I mentioned where words with the stem vowel *æ*, as in *dæg* and *fæt* equally affect adjectives such as *glæd* 'happy', although sometimes in marginally different ways. However, the material above is more than enough to allow you to understand the basic paradigms and, particularly, the contrast between the definite and indefinite declensions.

3.4 The verb 'to be'

So far I have simply ignored verb forms. I shall more fully repair this omission in the next two chapters, but by way of introduction I want here to look at parts of the paradigm of the verb 'to be'. There is a particular problem with this verb, of course, as there is in present-day English, which is that it is highly irregular. Compare with *be* a verb such as *love* with its past tense *loved*. However, the verb's irregularity is connected to another feature, namely its frequency. If you know any other languages than English, then it is almost certain that the same situation arises there too. I have already discussed the general issue of frequency earlier in this chapter, and therefore you should not be surprised or dismayed by the fact that the verb 'to be' is equally irregular in Old English. It is, if you like, a sign of the 'normality' of Old English.

The infinitive form of 'to be' in Old English is *bēon*, or (see further below) *wesan*, and the present tense indicative forms are as below. Note, however, that there are two parallel indicative paradigms. I shall explain these below:

	Present	
1 Sing.	eom	bēo
2 Sing.	eart	bist
3 Sing.	is	bið
Pl.	sindon	bēoð

Let me deal firstly with the 'double' paradigm. The first point to make is that both paradigms remained in existence until at least towards the end of the twentieth century, and indeed may still appear alongside each other. Many of you will have heard the usually fake 'Zummerzet' speech of south-west England, with forms such as *I be*, *he be* etc. These are relics of the second paradigm above. But everywhere else the first paradigm ousted the second, except, of course, in the infinitive, where *bēon* is today the only infinitive form. I shall explain the latter below.

The obvious question to ask about the above double paradigm is whether they represented, somehow, different meanings. The answer to that is in the affirmative, although the shades of meaning can merge together so that it is not always rigidly maintained. But we can say that the usual sense of the *eom* paradigm is to express a present state; *bēo*, on the other hand, is mostly used to express futurity or a timeless (generic) state.

In other respects the above paradigms are probably reasonably accessible. This is certainly true of the singular of the *eom* paradigm. There are, however, problems in the plural, where *sindon* is likely to be quite unfamiliar. It is, in fact, similar to forms in closely related languages such as Dutch *zijn* and German *sind*. The odd one out, as it were, is in fact present-day English *are*. There are, it has to be admitted, examples in Old English of *aron* 'they are' in northern and north-Midlands texts, but the interesting feature of these is that the form is not a native English one, but rather is due to Scandinavian influence.

This is indeed remarkable. When a language takes forms from another language, it is almost always the case that the **borrowed** or **loan** words are nouns, adjectives or verbs with full semantic meaning. This group of words is called **content** words, because of their semantic content. Opposed to these are **function** words, which have grammatical meaning rather than semantic or lexical meaning. Such words are rarely borrowed. I shall return to such questions of vocabulary in Chapter 8, but it does need to be noted that *aron* is an example of a function loan word.

The usual word *sindon* has other points which have to be addressed. Note especially that it is subject to considerable variation. Thus alongside *sindon* we find a short (and more original) form *sind*. Furthermore, as we have seen elsewhere, <i> alternates with <y>. And of course this is also true in *is*, where *ys* is common.

The paradigm of *bēo* is more straightforward, although, of course, *bist* will alternate with *byst*, although the latter is not so common. Otherwise it turns out that *bēo* is much more like 'normal' Old English verbs in its inflection, and therefore I shall postpone that discussion until Chapter 4.

The past indicative forms of 'to be' are very similar to the possibilities in present-day English, and it takes its forms from the alternative infinitive *wesan*:

	Past
1 Sing.	wæs
2 Sing.	wǣre
3 Sing.	wæs
Pl.	wǣron

The past tense is often described as the **preterite** in grammar books, but here I shall stick with the more common usage in present-day English, namely 'past'. Sometimes we find *was* rather than *wæs* but otherwise there is nothing of importance to note there.

One feature which is much more common in Old English than in present-day English is the use of special **subjunctive** forms. I shall attempt to explain the usage of the subjunctive in later chapters, but since it is so common, it is worth seeing the forms now:

Subjunctive	Present		Past
Sing.	sȳ	bēo	wǣre
Pl.	sȳn	bēon	wǣren

As can be seen, there is no distinction between the 1st, 2nd and 3rd persons, even in the singular. These special subjunctive forms are perhaps not quite as unusual as they might first appear to be, since you should already be familiar with present-day English phrases such as *If I were you...*

Finally, there are some further inflectional forms which correspond to forms also found today. There is both a present participle and a past participle. The former is either *wesende* or *bēonde*, whilst the latter is *ġebēon*. I shall explain the prefix *ġe-* in the next chapter. There are also two special forms for the imperative singular and plural: *wes* ~ *bēo* and *wesaδ* ~ *bēoδ*.

Exercise

Although it would be possible to present phrases which would test your ability to reproduce some of the material above, I don't believe that that approach works as well as giving you some real Old English to analyse. The exercise below follows the same pattern as that in Chapter 2, and again I have excerpted a passage from Ælfric, this time from the *Life of St. Mary of Egypt*:

And þǣr ġe-æt healfne dǣl þæs hlāfes	*there; ate; half; part*
and þæs wæteres ondranc and me þǣr on niht ġe-reste	*drank up; stayed*
and on ærne morġen ofer þā ēa fōr	*early morning; river went*
þā ongān iċ eft biddan mine lættewestran Sancta Maria	*began; again; pray; guide*
þæt hēo me ġe-rihte þyder hire willa wǣre	*direct; whither; willa*
Đus iċ becōm on þis wēsten	*arrived; wilderness*
and þanone oδ δisne andweardan dæġ	*since; until; present*
iċ feorrode symle flēonde minne God	*kept apart always; fleeing;*
anbīdiġende and ġe-hihtende	*awaiting; rejoicing*

The last line means: 'I have always been fleeing far away, awaiting my God and rejoicing in him'.

What I should like you to do is not merely to translate the passage into present-day English, preferably without using the glossary at the end of the book but merely using the glosses given above. I would also suggest that you should attempt to analyse the morphological structure of as many of the nouns and adjectives as you can. To do this you will have to seek the help of the glossary at the end, so try the translation first.

4 Verb forms

4.1 Verb types

In Old English, not wholly unlike present-day English, we can divide verbs up into three main groups, together with a handful of irregular verbs. The main groups are: (1) **weak verbs**; (2) **strong verbs**; (3) **modals**. But there are significant general differences which should be pointed out at once.

Firstly, you may have noticed that I have not suggested a group of auxiliary verbs parallel *to be, have* and *do*. For the last of these there is no problem, since *do* could only function as a full verb in Old English. It is arguable, however, that the first two could function rather like an **auxiliary**. At least for the present I shall, nevertheless, assume that their primary classification was as full verbs. This is quite easy to maintain in terms of morphology, but I shall come back to the issue in the chapters on syntax. And the category of modal auxiliary verbs, also, is far from identical in Old and present-day English. This is true both in terms of syntax and also morphology, and therefore it might seem perverse to claim a continuous category stretching from Old English to the present-day. Yet, as we shall see, there are common core characteristics whose continuous presence helps us also to understand the undoubted structural differences over time.

The first two groups, exemplified in present-day English by verbs such as *love* and *ride* respectively, cause fewer problems. The biggest change here is that the number and variety of strong verbs has declined steadily in the intervening period. One such example is *help*, which was a strong verb in Old English (and for some of the Middle English period too).

Turning now to the inflectional structure, what we shall find is that there is not the radical set of changes that occurred amongst the nouns and adjectives. This, it seems to me, makes the entry point for understanding verbs slightly less daunting than that for, say, nouns. Verbs inflect for the following features: person, tense and mood. Only the last will be at all unfamiliar. It refers to the inflections referring to the three **moods**, indicative, imperative and subjunctive and also to **voice**, to which I shall return shortly. I shall discuss the significance of each of these later, but for the moment we only need the briefest of notes. The **indicative** is what we might call the 'normal' mood. It gives the set of inflections which are used in ordinary declarative sentences and used everywhere except where some other inflection is required. It is, as it were, the default mood. The **imperative**, also, is probably familiar to you, although whereas in present-day English it is uninflected, in Old English it was inflected, as we shall see.

The subjunctive, however, may well be unfamiliar, although it is widely used in languages such as German and French. It is also used in, particularly, formal English, as in sentences such as *If I were you, I would do that*, where subjunctive *were* is used in preference to indicative *was*, a point I first noted in the previous chapter. In such usage the subjunctive is signalling that the conditional clause is not true or counterfactual. In broad terms we can say that in Old English the subjunctive is used not only in such cases but in a very wide range of cases where there is no claim that the clause or sentence is true. When we move on to syntax I shall come back to this quite complex issue.

Two paragraphs ago I implied that Old English presents no problems in respect of **tense**. Now it is true that, as today, there were only two sets of tense inflections, **present** and **past**, but this rather hides something. In present-day English there are special constructions for **aspect**, namely *be+ing* for progressive aspect and *have+ed* for perfective aspect, as in *I was walking* and *I have walked* respectively. These constructions are all-pervasive today, but although they existed in Old English they were not as common as today, and could have meanings different from those we associate with aspect. Furthermore, the use of *will/shall + verb* as a means of expressing the future is only at the stage of inception in Old English. Thus the Old English expression of tense is much simpler than that of today, and that should always be borne in mind. Of course, that is slightly misleading, for although the set of forms available is indeed simpler than in present-day English, there is a corresponding increase in the set of meanings which each tense has to cover.

Finally at this stage we should note that there was, with one exception, no morphological passive voice in Old English. The exception occurs with the verb *hātan* 'call' which has a passive form both singular (*hātte*) and plural (*hātton*), which is used in both the present and the past.

4.2 A weak verb

It is now time to look at the paradigm of a typical Old English verb. Let us firstly consider a weak verb. The reason for taking a weak rather than a strong verb first is that although the strong verbs have the older line of descent and contain a higher proportion of the core vocabulary, the weak verbs are most productive both in Old English and right up to the present-day. It also has to be said that they are, for the present-day reader, rather easier to grasp.

But the first point which has to be faced is that, just as nouns and adjectives have a variety of declensions, so verbs have a parallel variety of **conjugations**, that is to say, paradigm sets. This is not merely a matter of contrasts between weak and strong verbs; within each of these groups there are several different classes. In terms of weak verbs there are three classes, prosaically named as classes 1, 2 and 3. When we turn to strong verbs I shall distinguish these by using roman numerals, e.g. I, II, etc. This will help you to know immediately whether a verb is weak or strong.

When the paradigms for the weak conjugation are presented, the usual practice is to present them in numerical order. Here, however, I want to present the paradigm of a weak class 2 verb first, not out of awkwardness, but because it is the simplest. A typical verb of this conjugation is *lufian* 'love', and its paradigm is as follows:

	Present	Past
Present		
Indicative		
1 Sing.	lufie	lufode
2 Sing.	lufast	lufodest
3 Sing.	lufað	lufode
Plural	lufiað	lufodon
Subjunctive		
Sing.	lufie	lufode
Plural	lufien	lufoden
Imperative		
2 Sing.	lufa	————
2 Plural	lufiað	————
Participle	lufiende	ġelufod

There are no significant variations from this paradigm; note especially that heavy-stemmed verbs such as *lōcian* 'look' and *endian* 'end' follow exactly the same paradigm. The variations that do occur are found in unstressed syllables, so that, for example, there are many instances of *lufedon* rather than *lufodon*.

If we examine firstly the present tense, the 2nd and 3rd person forms persist until the time of the Authorised Bible, so perhaps they will be recognisable as related to *thou lovest* and *he/she/it loveth*. Present-day *he/she/it loves*, you should note, derives from *lufes* which already in Old English had become common in texts from the north-east of England, i.e. Northumbria, where we find, for example, *þu lufes, he lufes*. This is a point I shall return to in a later chapter. Such forms never appear in West Saxon texts of any period.

Another point to note is that in some parts of the paradigm there is an *-i-* after the stem, as in *lufie* whereas elsewhere there is no such vowel, as in *lufast*. This is not particularly important in itself, but it will be important when we compare class 2 verbs with class 1 verbs, so it is necessary to bear in mind its presence. Finally note the ending of the present particple *-iende*, for this is quite different from the present-day ending *-ing*. In fact the origin of the present-day ending is somewhat muddy, and it appears to be due to a coalescence of a variety of different morphological and dialect forms, all brought together by the merger of unstressed forms which is a significant feature of Middle English.

Moving on to the past tense forms, most of these should be quite transparent, with the single exception of the past participle, where there is a prefixed element *ġe-*. This prefix is not completely obligatory, but it is present almost all of the time. Furthermore, it occurs equally when the participle is used as an verbal adjective as well as in its more purely verbal context. There has been much argument about the proper nomenclature for the past participle, which here we can easily ignore. Beyond noting that the past participle is part of the paradigm of every verb (including *bēon/wesan* with past participle *ġewesen*), it should also be observed that the prefix remains in use until about the time of Chaucer, by which time it has been reduced to *y-*, as in *yclept* 'called'.

4.3 More weak verbs

Let us turn our attention to weak class 1 verbs. Here there is a distinction which needs to be observed between verbs with a short stem vowel and a long one. Let me start off with an example of the former, *trymman* 'strengthen':

Present		Past
Indicative		
1 Sing.	trymme	trymede
2 Sing.	trymest	trymedest
3 Sing.	trymeð	trymede
Plural	trymmað	trymedon

Subjunctive

Sing.	trymme	trymede
Plural	trymmen	trymedon

Imperative

2nd Sing.	tryme	_____
2nd Plural	trymmað	_____

Participle	trymmende	ġetrymed

Much is similar here to class 2, but there are subtle differences, as in the inflection of the 2nd and 3rd person singular. But the biggest difference of all comes in the shape of the present tense as a whole. You should have observed that sometimes there is a double consonant, sometimes a single. This is no mere variation in spelling. I mentioned the contrast between single and double, or geminate, consonants in Chapter 1, and here we see a situation where the contrast is crucial. For example, it is only that contrast which demonstrates the difference between 1 Sing. indicative and the singular subjunctive, i.e. *trymme ~ tryme*.

Gemination plays a further role in the two conjugations I have discussed so far. If you look more carefully at the two present tense paradigms and compare them one by one, then you may notice something rather interesting. Everywhere that the class 1 verb has a geminate consonant the corresponding class 2 verb has -*i*-, and everywhere that the class 1 verb has only a single consonant the class 2 verb has no medial -*i*-. The historical explanation of this is rather complex, but one of the critical features is that the process of gemination must have been a sound change which occurred at a pre-historic period in the development of the language, but one which could not affect class 2 verbs.

Unlike class 2 verbs, the class 1 verbs show quite a lot of further variation, but I shall delay my discussion of that until later. Instead let us now turn our attention to class 1 verbs with heavy stem syllables. Below I give the paradigm of *dēman* 'judge, deem', a typical such verb:

Present		*Past*
Indicative		
1 Sing.	dēme	dēmde
2 Sing.	dēmst	dēmdest
3 Sing.	dēmð	dēmde
Plural	dēmað	dēmdon
Subjunctive		
Sing	dēme	dēmde
Plural	dēmen	dēmdon

Imperative

2nd Sing.	dēm	_____
2nd Plural	dēmað	_____

| *Participle* | dēmende | ġedēmed |

Given the discussion immediately above, the first thing to note is that here there is no sign of gemination. The reason for that is that gemination could only occur after a light syllable. This mention of syllable weight leads us on naturally to the next point. Forms such as *dēmst, dēmð, dēmde* do not have any vowel immediately after the stem, in contrast to all the other forms we have encountered. This is the result of a process called **syncope**. Broadly speaking, what happens is that a fully unstressed vowel is lost after a heavy syllable provided that it is followed by further syllabic material. Of course, this does not immediately appear to be the case in *dēmst* and *dēmð*; compare *ġedēmed* where there is no syncope. All that I can say here, rather unsatisfactorily, is that at the time when the change occurred, there was indeed a further following vowel. Despite this, the actual process of syncope is not too difficult to understand, especially because it can happen in later periods of English too. That explains, for example, the pronunciation of *business*, where there are only two syllables, compare *busyness* 'the state of being busy', where there is no syncope.

There is a slight glitch in the conjugation of class 1 verbs which I have yet to mention. This occurs in conjugation of verbs with a light stem ending in -*r*. Since the glitch is apparent only in the present tense, we need only examine those forms. An example of such a verb is *nerian* 'save':

Present

Indicative		*Subjunctive*	
1 Sing.	nerie		
2 Sing.	nerest		
3 Sing.	nereð	Sing.	nerie
Plural	neriað	Plural	nerien
Imperative			
2nd Sing.	nere	2nd Plural	neriað
Participle	neriende		

Why do these forms differ from the usual short-stemmed verbs, and how do they do so? The answer to the second of these questions helps to answer the first. For it should be clear that the distinguishing feature of these verbs is that they show medial -*i*- in exactly where they should have a geminate consonant. Although there is no completely adequate explanation of why /r/ should prevent gemination, it is undoubtedly the case that it does so.

There is an interesting consequence of this failure. As you can see, verbs like *nerian* fall halfway between class 1 and class 2 verbs, in not having gemination but rather preserving *-i-*; on the other hand they otherwise have the typical class 1 inflexions, e.g. *nereð* rather than those of class 2, compare *lufað*. Old English speakers appear to have noticed that state of affairs too and consequently in later texts, such as those from the period of Ælfric, words such as *nerian* began to adopt the inflections of the class 2 conjugation so that we find *nerað* as well as *nereð*. This is an early sign of what was to come, when in the Middle English period simplification to one weak verb class occurred.

4.4 Unmutated verbs

There was in Old English a small but important group of verbs which were in origin part of class 1 but which had already undergone drastic modification. Historical grammars always classify these verbs as belonging to a sub-group of class 1, but there is good reason for not doing so. I shall call these verbs 'unmutated verbs', an ugly terms derived from the German term *Rückumlaut* 'reverse umlaut'. I shall explain more about this phenomenon, which involves the sound change called *i*-umlaut which I referred to when discussing nouns like *fōt* 'foot' in the previous chapter, in §4.5. A typical unmutated verb is *sellan* 'sell'. In the present tense such a verb is exactly like any other class 1 verb, but its past tense is very different:

	Present	Past
Indicative		
1 Sing.	selle	sealde
2 Sing.	selest	sealdest
3 Sing.	seleð	sealde
Plural	sellað	sealdon
Subjunctive		
Sing.	selle	sealde
Plural	sellen	sealdon
Imperative		
2nd Sing.	sele	_____
2nd Plural	sellað	
Participle	sellende	ġeseald

As you can see, the stem vowel of the past is unexpected given what we have seen so far. But it is also true that we find the same kind of alternation in present-day English *sell* ~ *sold*. That is why I have chosen to assign such verbs to a class of their own. Today there is only one verb which follows the same pattern, namely *tell* = Old English *tellan*, but there were others in Old English: *cwellan* 'kill', *dwellan* 'dwell', *stellan* 'place'.

There is, however, another group of verbs which belong to the same conjugation, such as *bringan* ~ *brōhte* 'bring'. You may have noted that all the verbs in the previous paragraph have a stem which in the past participle ends in *-l-* followed directly by the regular suffixal consonant *-d*. In the case of all the verbs in this second group the sequence we find is always *-ht*. This group, although also small in number, includes a significant number of easily recognised words, such as *bycġan* ~ *bohte* 'buy', *þyncan* ~ *pōhte* 'think', *sēcan* ~ *sōhte* 'seek', together with several other word which have either become once more regular or have been lost: *læċċan* 'catch', *streċċan* 'stretch', *þeċċan* 'cover, thatch', *þynċan* 'seem', *weċċan* 'wake', *wyrċan* 'work' and a few others. Occasionally we find remnants of the Old English system in the present-day language, for example *wrought* from *wyrċan*.

This conjugation is of interest, of course, because it remains salient, albeit small, in the present-day language. It is even the case that since the Old English period one important verb, borrowed from French and therefore, as a loan word, originally entirely regular, has in time gone over to this declension. This is the word *catch*, compare French *chasser* 'chase'.

4.5 A phonological interlude

In Chapter 3 I discussed the mutation declension, as in *man* ~ *men*, and now I have discussed 'unmutated' weak verbs. You may have guessed that the two classes have something in common. Indeed, you may have noted that they share an alternation on the one hand between (crudely speaking) singular and plural and on the other hand between present and past, in which the crucial feature is that the stem vowel changes. The change works rather differently in the two paradigms, but nevertheless the principles are the same, and since there are clear instances of the consequences for both in the present-day language, it is worth spending a little time on the issue.

The change reflects a sound change which occurred at an early time in the Old English period thus prior to the appearance of any of our major texts; it is also found in other Germanic languages such as

German. The sound change is known either as **i-umlaut** or **i-mutation** the two terms being interchangeable. For those of you who know German it will be familiar to you from words such as *Mann* ~ *Männer* (in German the double dots over the *a* in *Männer* is known as an *Umlaut*).

I-mutation was caused when there was either an /i/ or a /j/ in the final syllable of a word, for this /i/ (or /j/, but I shall not separately mention again /j/ for the sake of brevity) influenced the vowel in the immediately preceding syllable, with the effect that the vowel was fronted if originally back or raised if it was already fronted. The effects can be displayed in a simple diagram:

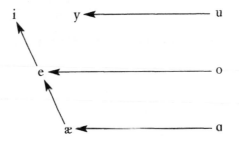

In the case of the back vowels the change affected both long and short vowels, whereas only short front vowels were affected. Additionally, in the case of the low and short back vowel /ɑ/ it usually has a further raising to /e/.

Some time after i-mutation occurred the /i/ which caused the change was either lost or changed into /e/, so that we can see the following progression, exemplified in the plural of *gōs* 'goose':

gōsi- > gēsi- > gēs

Other examples from the mutation declension, showing the change with a range of vowels, include: *mūsī* > *mȳs* 'mice', *hnuti* > *hnyte* 'nuts', *burig* > *byrg* 'castles', *manni* > *mænn* > *menn* 'people', *āci* > *ǣċ* 'oaks'. Note how the front vowel corresponding to /u/ is /y/, never /i/. In fact the majority of instances of stressed ȳ in Old English are due in one way or another to the influence of i-mutation. There are some other elements in a full description of i-mutation, most notably that existing diphthongs are equally affected by the change. I shall return to that point at a later stage.

Although the above will help you to understand the mutation declension of nouns, none of the above quite explains the unmutated conjugation of weak verbs. The best place to start here is with the regular class 1 conjugation. Recall the typical example *trymman*. Given what I said in the last sentence of the previous paragraph, you should be able to tell that the vowel of the stem vowel is the result of i-mutation. This is true of every regular class 1 verb, including both the types *dēman* and *nerian*. In most cases the /i/ which causes the mutation is lost, but that is not so in the case of *nerian*. And in the past the /i/ remained but then changed to /e/, hence *trymede*. In class 2 verbs, however, there is never any i-mutation, and the *i* which appears in, say, *lufian* was not present before i-mutation occurred.

In unmutated verbs the present tense is exactly like any other class 1 verb. Thus *sellan* comes from earlier *salljan* (via *sællan*), just as *trymman* comes from *trummjan*. But in the past tense the /i/ which causes mutation was lost before the change took place (or perhaps was never there in the first place). It is in that sense that these verbs are called unmutated verbs; the German term *Rückumlaut* implies that these verbs never had an *i* between the stem and the inflexion.

I-mutation is a process which is virtually all-pervasive in Old English, and we shall see further examples of its importance at later points in this work. It is, therefore, important that you have some understanding of its role in Old English. But, as I have shown, it also remains an influence on our language even today.

4.6 More weak verbs

There are four further weak verbs which historically belong to a third conjugation, which at one stage contained many more words. These are *habban* 'have', *libban* 'love', *seċġan* 'say' and *hyċġan* 'think'. In Old English the class 3 verbs look rather like a mixture of class 1 and class 2, having class 1 features such as gemination and i-mutation (but not throughout in the latter case) alongside several class 2 inflections.

The result of this, when combined with the fact that all four verbs, and most of all *habban*, are of very high frequency and set against the isolated character of the conjugation, means, almost inevitably, that there is a great deal of variation in form. I present below a paradigm for *habban*, but only in the context of that last point:

Present		*Past*
Indicative		
1 Sing.	hæbbe	hæfde
2 Sing.	hæfst	hæfdest
3 Sing.	hæfð	hæfde
Plural	habbað	hæfdon

Subjunctive

Sing.	hæbbe	hæfde
Plural	hæbben	hæfden

Imperative

2 Sing.	hafa	_____
2 Plural	habbað	_____
Participle	hæbbende	ġehæfd

There are several points which still have to be made. Firstly, in terms of gemination the alternation is not simply between a single and a double consonant, but between <f> and <bb> in the cases of *habban* and *libban*, and between <g> and <ċġ> in *seċġan* and *hyċġan*. This alternation is not specific to these verbs, but occurs wherever there is an possible alternation within these two pairs. Secondly, i-mutation is often found in a rather confused pattern, as a result of other forms, notably from class 2 forms where, of course, there is no i-mutation. Thirdly, one of the characteristic features of class 3 verbs is that they have much more syncope of unstressed vowels than we have seen elsewhere.

4.7 'Anomalous' verbs

In Chapter 3 we looked at the verb *bēon/wesan*, which fits into no other category. There are three other verbs similarly isolated and whose origin is complex and well beyond the scope of this work. Traditionally these verbs are called anomalous verbs, because their structures are unlike those of any other verb type. The verbs in question are: *willan* 'will', *dōn* 'do' and *gān* 'go'. Their idiosyncratic behaviour, although well-defined, is best shown by simply presenting their paradigms in a rather brief form:

Pres.	*willan*	*dōn*	*gān*
1 Sing.	wille	dō	gā
2 Sing.	wilt	dēst	gǣst
3 Sing.	wile	dēð	gǣð
Plural	willað	dōð	gāð
Subj. (Pl.)	wille (willen)	dō (dōn)	gā (gān)
Participle	willende	dōnde	_____
Past			
Ind.	wolde	dyde	ēode
Participle	_____	ġedōn	ġegān

All the other forms can be simply deduced. In the past tense you should take a verb form such as *dēmde* as the base.

Of the above forms, the past tense form of *gān*, namely *ēode*, is probably the one that stands out as being odd, as quite unrelated to present-day English and at the same time unlike any of the other Old English forms. This is the result of **suppletion**. In suppletion what happens is that some forms in the paradigm are taken from one lexical word (in this case *gān*) and other forms are taken from an entirely different lexical word (here *ēode*). Interestingly for the history of English, the past tense suppletive forms were replaced in Middle English by an alternative suppletion, based on the past tense of *wend*, so that *went* took over from *ēode*. That in turn caused *wend* to form a new past tense of its own, the regular form *wended*.

4.8 More on i-mutation and suppletion and adjectives

Now that we have spent a little time on the topics of i-mutation and suppletion, the opportunity has arrived to bring these two topics together by looking once more at adjectives. When we discussed adjectives in Chapter 3, the one major issue I completely ignored was the method used in Old English to produce **comparative** and **superlative** forms.

For the most part there are no serious difficulties here when the forms are compared with those in present-day English. Note, especially, that **comparison** by the use of *more, most* with the **positive** adjective is virtually non-existent in Old English, and all forms are derived by inflection. Note also that all comparatives are declined only according to the definite declension; this is because comparative forms are inherently definite. Superlatives have some indefinite inflections but not throughout the paradigm.

For the majority of adjectives, therefore, the process of comparison is achieved by the addition of standard comparative and superlative suffixes. The comparative suffix is *-ra*, the superlative suffix is *-ost*. Thus the compared forms of the definite adjective *blinda* 'blind' are *blindra, blindost*. The most common variation here occurs with a small group of adjectives which have a final *-u* in the positive, for example *calu* 'bald', *ġearu* 'ready', *mearu* 'tender', *nearu* 'narrow', which have forms of the type *nearora, nearwost*, which reflects the fact that historically they originate from an otherwise lost declension.

But there are some important adjectives which do not follow the above patterns. There can be two quite separate reasons for this. The first, and larger, group consists of adjectives which had compared forms deriving from a different form of the two inflections, namely a shape in which the inflections originally started with an *i*. This *i* appears as an *e* in the superlative but disappears altogether from the comparative. But, more importantly, before it disappears it causes i-mutation in the compared forms of the relevant adjective. A typical example of this is *eald* 'old' with compared forms *yldra*, *yldest*. Other similar adjectives are: *feorr* 'far', *grēat* 'great', and *sċeort* 'short', whilst *lang* 'long' and *strang* 'strong' differ only in having *e* as the mutation vowel, e.g. *lengra*, although if you refer back to the previous section you will see that that is to be expected, whilst *ġeong* 'young' has *ġingra*, *ġingest*. Two further adjectives, *brāda* 'broad' and *hēah* 'high', have both mutated forms and the normal comparison as in *blinda*, whilst *nēah* 'near' has an unmutated comparative and a mutated superlative.

The type of variation seen in those last three words quite probably indicate that these i-mutated forms were always in competition with the unmutated regular variety, and this suggestion is supported by the fact that in present-day English they have all lost their mutated forms with the exception of *elder*, *eldest* alongside *older*, *oldest*. But even then the mutated forms are of restricted usage.

The second group is smaller, but contains items of the highest frequency. I have not mentioned these previously because their shared feature is suppletion. There are only four words here, which split into two semantic groups. The first of these comprises the words *gōd* 'good' and *yfel* 'evil, bad'; the second consists of *lytel* 'little' and *miċel* 'large'. The paradigm each is as follows:

gōd	betra ~ sēlra	betst ~ sēlest
yfel	wyrsa	wyrst
lytel	lǣssa	lǣst
miċel	māra	mǣst

Note that in the case of *gōd* there is not one set of suppletive forms but two. There is no distinction to be made between them. When the equivalent adverbs, *well*, *yfle*, *lyt* and *miċle*, are used they also have suppletive forms.

Exercise

The following passage is taken from Bede's account of Cædmon, often called the first English poet. Bede was a monk writing at the beginning of the eighth century and based in northern County Durham. His greatest work was the *Historia Ecclesiastica Gentis Anglorum* or 'The Ecclesiastical History of the English People'. Bede has the best claim to be the first systematic historian of Britain and, without chauvinism, it can be claimed that in the first half of the eighth century Northumbria was the intellectual centre of Western Europe.

It is often claimed, on the basis of Bede's *History*, that Cædmon was the first poet of English, although such a claim has nothing like the substance we can attach to Bede himself. Cædmon was an apparently illiterate farm-worker attached to the Abbey of Whitby during the abbacy of Hilda between 650 and 679. The story tells of how this farm-worker was inspired by a divine dream to compose a religious poem, a commonplace theme in medieval literature. At least as interesting as this is the point that Hilda was Abbess of a 'double' house, i.e. one containing both monks and nuns.

I have chosen the following passage, which follows the discovery of Cædmon's songwriting skills, not because of its literary interest, but more prosaically: because it contains quite a number of weak verbs! You will also observe that the linguistic forms in this text sometimes differ slightly from those seen either in the paradigms I have presented or those you have seen in the texts extracted from Ælfric. The original Bede manuscript was written in Latin, of course, but it was later translated into Old English, the most reliable manuscript (Tanner 10, Bodleian Library) being of the second half of the tenth century, but containing various forms which are dialectally distinct from those used by Ælfric. This may seem a nuisance, but it is a good idea to begin the confrontation with variant forms as early as possible. As before, I have glossed most of the words you will find unfamiliar.

Ðā onġan sēo abbudisse clyppan ond lufiġean þa Godes ġife in þǣm men;	*began; accept; grace*
ond hēo hine þā monade ond lǣrde þæt hē worulhād anforlēte ond	*urge; instruct; secular life; renounce*
munuchād onfēnġ; ond hē þæt wel þafode.	*monastic life; accept; agree to*
Ond hēo hine in þæt mynster onfēnġ mid his gōdum ond hine ġeþēodde	*monastery; with; goods; receive*
to ġesomnunge þāra Godes þēowa ond heht hine lǣran þæt ġetæl	*company; servant; order; teach; tale*
þæs hālgan stǣres ond spelles.	*holy; history; message*
Ond hē eal þā hē in ġehyrnesse ġeleornian meahte mid hine ġemyngade,*	*hearing; learn; could; remember*
ond swā swā clǣne nēten eodorcende in þæt swēteste lēoð ġehwerfde.	*just like pure cattle chewing cud; sweetest song; turn*
Ond his song ond his lēoð wǣron swā wynsumu to ġehyranne þætte	*joyful; that*

seolfan þā lārēowas æt his mūðe wreoton ond leornodon.   *self, teacher; voice; write*

* 'And everything he could learn through hearing he remembered in his head'

5 Strong verbs

5.1 Present-day English

When we look at present-day English we find many verbs which pattern in a very similar way to the weak verbs of Old English, even if there has been some obvious simplification: for example there are no longer two major classes, for they have merged together, so that an Old English class 1 verb *cyssan* 'kiss' and a class 2 verb such as *lufian* 'love', now pattern in parallel.

On the other hand there are a number of verbs, other than any of those I have discussed above, which do not show any of the distinguishing features of a weak verb. In particular, these verbs do not have the characteristic past tense inflection of the weak verbs and, furthermore, they show an apparently arbitrary variation in their stem in order to indicate their past tense and participle forms. Such is what we find in a verb such as *sing*, with past tense *sang* and past participle *sung*.

In English today these verbs are often classed as irregular verbs, but they are, in most cases, directly derivable from what are called the **strong** verbs of Old English. This rather implies that what now seems to be a rather unpredictable variation in the present-day language has not always been so, and that, for example, the Old English verb *singan* 'sing' had a predictable variation in form. Our first task, therefore, will be to analyse the state of affairs in Old English and then to see how that might help us to understand the present-day variations also.

5.2 Ablaut

In heading this section of Chapter 5 with the term **Ablaut**, I am conscious that this will look like a reference back to Umlaut. There is, indeed, a distant similarity, but that is best ignored. I use the German term because the equivalent English one, **vowel gradation**, is regrettably clumsy.

The best way to approach Ablaut is by starting with a present-day verb like *sing*. I have already shown that this verb has three basic shapes, which we can display as a simple paradigm:

Present	*Past*	*Past Participle*
sing	sang	sung

As we look at this verb it becomes immediately apparent that the only thing that distinguishes one part of this verb from another is the shape of the vowel, whether it is /ɪ/, /æ/ or /ʌ/, and there is no sign of a distinct inflectional suffix. Of course we can add one in certain contexts, as in *she sings*, but that has no effect on which vowel is used, so that *she sang* is the corresponding past tense form and there is no inflectional suffix at all, since no such suffix is available for this verb in that part of the paradigm.

If, in strong verbs, there are no inflectional suffixes which distinguish present and past tenses, how is it possible to know when a verb is present or past? The only possible answer to this question has to be that the past tense (and the past participle also) are distinguished by the variation in stem vowel. And this is not a mere idiosyncrasy of the verb *sing*. There are other verbs which behave identically, for example *ring* and *swim*. But there are other verbs which have the same basic pattern but where the pattern is different and this seems to be because the stem vowel is different. An example of this would be *ride* with the past tense form *rode*.

Thus what we can observe is a patterned variation in stem vowel which has the function of carrying information about, in particular, features associated with tense. It is this patterned variation which is known as Ablaut. Ablaut is a feature which is found throughout the Germanic languages and is indeed one of the defining features of these languages. With the lapse of time its presence is not always obvious and it can, for example, be tempting to suppose that every present-day verb which shows vowel variation between the present and the past is an example of a strong verb. But as we have already seen, in Chapter 4, the examples of the unumlauting verbs such as *sell* show this to be false. There are, regrettably, other examples where later changes occur and muddy the waters further. In Old English, however, the position is usually much clearer.

5.3 Strong verb classes

I have already shown that in present-day English there are several other verbs which follow the same pattern as *sing*. Let's call this an Ablaut pattern. Consider now another present-day verb, *ride*, which I mentioned two paragraphs ago. This too shows an Ablaut pattern: *ride ~ rode ~ ridden* (ignore for a moment the *-en* suffix). It will be clear, however, that this pattern is not the same as that in *sing*. One way of confirming this is by noting that the two patterns do not rhyme.

The same situation holds in Old English, and it results from the fact that the Ablaut patterns derive from a much earlier stage in the development of the language. This, of course, explains why all the Germanic languages share Ablaut. There were, in fact, six Ablaut patterns in Germanic, and a further group of verbs which share this pattern in complex and obscure ways. It is therefore usual to talk about seven strong verb classes (the six more or less regular classes plus the seventh more obscure class). There is no reason to depart from this description here and I shall henceforth talk about class I, class II, etc. Note that I use Roman numbers as a mnemonic to distinguish strong verbs from the weak verbs.

Let us start our examination of strong verbs with a typical class I verb, *rīdan* 'ride'. In Old English, as opposed to today, there are always four possible ablaut variations. These are usually exemplified from the infinitive, past tense singular, past tense plural and the past participle. Thus the paradigm of *rīdan* is as follows:

Infinitive	Past Sing.	Past Pl.	Past Part.
rīdan	rād	ridon	ġeriden

The most important warning to issue here is that the references to 'past singular' and 'past plural' are misleading. 'Past singular' refers only to special forms for the 1st and 3rd singular of the indicative, i.e. the equivalents of *I rode* and *he/she/it rode*. Every other past tense form follows the shape of what I have called the 'past plural'.

A comparison of the full paradigm of a verb such as *drīfan* with, say, *dēman*, shows a number of distinctions between weak and strong verbs:

		Past
Present		
Indicative		
1 Sing.	drīfe	drāf
2 Sing.	drīfst	drife
3 Sing.	drīfð	drāf
Plural	drīfað	drifon
Subjunctive		
Sing.	drīfe	drife
Plural	drīfen	drifen

Imperative
2nd Sing.   drīf   ————
2nd Plural   drīfað   ————
Participle   drīfende   ġedrifen

Within the present tense the differences which appear in the 2nd sing. and 3rd sing. are more apparent than real. They arise out of the process of syncope which I discussed when dealing with *dēman* in §4.2. This should not cause you any difficulties in the paradigm above. However, in many other verbs, such as *rīdan*, the process of syncope would have produced *rīdst, rīdð*. This quite often results in awkward sequences of consonants and therefore various types of assimilation, that is to say, the process of making different consonants more or completely similar, occurs. Assimilation changes the sequence to *rītst, rītt*. Similarly from 'expected' *bītð* 'it bites' we get *bītt*.

The real differences occur in the past tense and past participle forms. I have already mentioned that the 1st and 3rd singular indicative forms are quite different from any of the others. Note now that this extends to the fact that there is no inflectional suffix at all in these two forms, which thus contrast with the weak verbs. Of course the major contrast between the past tense forms of weak and strong verbs is represented by the fact that in all weak verbs there is a suffix intervening between the stem and the inflectional ending. This suffixal ending always contains a /d/ or, less often, a /t/. As a result it is customary to call this a dental suffix. This is a primary feature of weak verbs which is entirely absent from strong verbs. For strong verbs the inflectional endings are added directly to the stem, and this accounts, for example, for the past plural form *drifon*, compare *dēmdon*, where the dental suffix -*d*- is apparent.

Another quite small difference occurs in the 2nd sing., which does not have the -*st* inflection found elsewhere. Of much more interest, however, is the past participle. In all strong verbs the inflection of this participle is always -*en*. This is often, but not always, paralleled in the present-day language. Thus, for example, the past participle of *sing* is today *sung*, but in Old English it was *ġesungen*. Any of you who know either Dutch or German will immediately realise that in this respect Old English, Dutch and German are entirely parallel.

All strong verbs inflect in much the same way, regardless of which class they belong to, but below I shall mention some of the more important variations which are found. But the fact that, unlike the weak verbs, strong verbs cohere as a group in terms of inflection means that we can proceed for the moment on a different track. From everything I have said above it should be clear that the differences between different classes of strong verbs are a matter of different ablaut patterns. Let us, therefore, look at the pattern found in each class:

I	drīfan	drāf	drifon	-drifen 'drive'
II	smēocan	smēac	smucon	-smocen 'smoke'
III	singan	sanc	suncon	-suncen 'sink'
IV	beran	bær	bǣron	-boren 'bear'
V	sprecan	sprǣc	sprǣcon	-sprecen 'speak'

As it stands, the display above is unhelpful. It looks like no more than a more complex version of what we find today. That may well be true, but it is possible to make more sense of the situation. For although by the Old English period the original ablaut patterns had been considerably obscured by the passage of time (and sound change), it is possible to reconstruct what the situation might have been like in Germanic. And in so doing some remarkable features emerge.

Recall now that the defining feature of Ablaut is the stem, or, more accurately, root vowel. If we take a class I verb and analyse it as containing an **onset**, a **nucleus** and a **coda**, that is to say, a set of initial consonants, a vocalic nucleus and a set of final consonants, then we can define, say, *drīfan*, as: /dr/ + /iː/ + /f/ (ignoring the inflection as irrelevant). It will be obvious that the crucial element is the nucleus. We still have some work to do, and the essential business consists of a two-stage process. Firstly, instead of saying that there is a long vowel in the nucleus, let us say that there are two short vowels, i.e. /i + i/. This is quite a common analysis of long vowels in phonological theory, so it is quite acceptable here too. The second stage will appear more mysterious, but what I propose to do is to label the two vowels differently. I shall call the first vowel the Ablaut vowel, or A (for Ablaut), and the second vowel a contextual element, or X. That may seem mysterious, but it should be recalled that we have already seen that Ablaut is the defining feature of strong verbs, and thus what I am doing is claiming that Ablaut is not just something in the ether, but rather has overt expression.

Having done this analysis, then we can say that *drīfan* actually has an internal structure of Onset + Nucleus + Coda and that the Nucleus consists of Ablaut vowel + some defined context, as I shall show very shortly. The structure of the onset is generally irrelevant, but we do need to show any coda structure. It is true that in some cases, including class I, it would not seem necessary to invoke any reference to the coda. That is not wholly true even in that class, although the argument would require me to get involved in matters to do with the earliest stage of Indo-European. However, it will shortly become clear that elements of the coda can indeed be crucial, so it seems most helpful to indroduce the concept even here.

Let me show how the Ablaut system works in practice:

drīf-	drāf-	drif-	drif-
-AXC-	-AXC-	-AXC-	-AXC-
-eiC-	-aiC-	-ØiC-	-ØiC-

It can be seen that the contextual element is /i/ and that it remains constant. It is this contextual element which is the defining feature of the different verb classes. On the other hand, the Ablaut element varies, appearing as either /e/ or /a/ or Ø (zero). The reason for this is that Ablaut is subject to two types of gradation (hence the English term vowel gradation). There is **qualitative gradation**, which occurs when one vowel replaces another. The variation always involves variation between /e/ and /a/, so that is the explanation for the alternation between -*ei*- and -*ai*-. There is also **quantitative gradation**; in the examples above this is realised as variation between a normal length vowel and either Ø or a reduced vowel similar to the initial of present-day *about*. This reduced vowel is often called **schwa** and it has some variation, but I shall use /ə/ when needed. So, still schematically, we can describe the ablaut pattern above as: front ~ back ~ reduced ~ reduced. The other variations from Old English which can be seen above, namely the monophthongisation of /ei/ to /iː/ and of /ai/ to /aː/ are quite separate developments in English, nothing to do with Ablaut, but belonging to the pre-history of Old English and rather outside this book.

All this may seem rather random, perhaps to the extent of being quite unhelpful. But compare with the Ablaut series above the corresponding series for class II verbs:

smēoc-	smēac	smuc-	smoc-
-AXC-	-AXC-	-AXC-	-AXC-
-euC-	-auC-	-ØuC-	-ØuC-

The only significant difference between the two series is that the contextual element has changed from /i/ to /u/. Of course, as before, the situation is obscured by other Old English developments. But, rather than concentrate on those, the general principle, that the main shift between different classes is caused by the contextual element which immediately follows the ablauting vowel, should be recognised as the critical feature.

The distinguishing feature of class III verbs is that the context is either a liquid (/l, r/) or a nusal (/m, n/), which are classed together as sonorants (S). Thus we find:

sing-	sang	sung-	sung-
-AXC-	-AXC-	-AXC-	-AXC-
-eSC-	-aSC-	-əSC-	-əSC-

Note that I have used schwa rather than zero, for here the ablaut vowel surfaces as /u/, rather than disappearing.

So far I have suggested that there are two ablaut grades: normal and reduced. However, it is also possible to find a lengthened grade, where the normal vowel becomes long. This happens in classes IV and V, where the past plural has lengthened grade (and also, qualitatively, *a*-grade). Thus in class IV we find the following; note that I have specified the context as a sonorant:

ber-	bær	bǣr-	bor-
-AS-	-AS-	-AAS-	-AS-
-eS-	-aS-	-eeS-	-əS-

Here and in class V there are, as elsewhere, some particular Old English developments. Otherwise class V is parallel to class IV except that the final element is an obstruent (O), i.e. a 'true' consonant, rather than a sonorant, and this affects the final shape of the schwa vowel:

sprec-	spræc	sprǣc-	sprec-
-AO-	-AO-	-AAO-	-AO-
-eO-	-aO-	-eeO-	-əO-

It would be possible to extend this analysis of Ablaut to class VI, but this would involve an extremely complex and not necessarily rewarding discussion. Instead, therefore, I simply present a typical example:

VI	faran	fōr	fōron	-faren 'go'

So far I have ignored class VII verbs, although they are often of quite high frequency. My reason for this is that they do not fit in to the ablaut series proper and are of varied origin. Nor is it possible, as it is with other strong verbs, to determine the class by reference to their infinitive. The best means of identifying these verbs is by their past tense forms, where they all have stem vowel *ēo* or, less often, *ē*. Typical examples of each time are shown below:

VII (a)	feallan	fēoll	fēollon	-feallan 'go'
(b)	hātan	hēt	hēton	-hāten 'call'

The overwhelming majority of these verbs also have the same stem vowel in the past participle as in the infinitive.

5.4 Variation in strong verbs

As I have hinted at, there are a number of areas where there is variation both within and across strong verb classes. This should not be surprising, for these are, historically, of longer lineage than the weak verbs, and therefore there was greater time in which variation could arise. It is impossible here to account for all this variation, and I shall restrict myself to the most important of the changes.

An obvious place to start is with i-mutation. In strong verbs i-mutation is evident in the 2nd and 3rd person singular present forms. Of course not every strong verb is affected: for example most class I are unaffected, since their stem vowel is *ī*. It is always found with classes II, VI and VII, and a technically different, although in practice identical, shift of *e* to *i* in classes IV and V has exactly the same effect, so that we find *beran* 'bear' but *birst* 'thou bearest'. Some other sound changes in the development of the language can also cause some minor variations in the stem vowel, so that, for example, we find class III *helpan* 'help' with stem vowel *e* which then can be subject to i-mutation to give *hilpst* in a fairly transparent way. I am not going to discuss most of these changes, which would merely muddy the waters unnecessarily.

There is a small group of verbs in classes V and VI which form their present tense in the same way as weak class 1 verbs, e.g. *sittan* 'sit' V, *hlihhan* 'laugh' VI. The temptation is to see these 'weak presents' as fore-runners of the later gradual shift of many strong verbs to the weak system, but that temptation should be resisted. Note, for example, that although *laugh* is indeed weak today, *sit* is strong.

There are some other verbs which also have paradigms which are irregular from a morphological point of view. Amongst these are the following. Firstly there are some class II verbs which have an unexpected *-ū-* in their present tense, e.g. *brūcan* 'enjoy'. It is probable that the source of this is analogical. That is to say, the present tense has no phonological explanation, but rather it would appear that the small group of verbs involved adopted new stem vowels on the analogy of class I. There the past plural stem vowel *drifon* appears to be a short version of the *ī* in the infinitive *drīfan*: this sets up a proportion ī : i. Applying that to class II we get the following statement: ī : i :: X : u, and X is satisfied only by ū. Analogy is a concept which is often used almost wantonly in historical studies, but this example is one that shows that it can be used legitimately if the criteria for its application are sufficiently tightly drawn. Finally on this group of verbs, it can be noted that the same, or virtually the same, verbs in other Germanic languages show the same phenomenon; compare German *brauchen* or Dutch *gebruiken*, where the respective diphthongs *-au-* and *-ui-* represent the development of original *-u-*.

In class III there are few verbs like *berstan* 'burst' and *breġdan* 'pull' which must be mentioned, if only because some textbooks characterise this type as demonstrating the basic paradigm for the class. But if you refer back to the discussion of Ablaut it will be clear from what is said there that these verbs do not properly belong to class III. In fact they were originally class V verbs which at some stage acquired an additional element which disrupted their paradigm and hence they shifted to a more appropriate ablaut series.

Before I conclude the discussion of strong verbs by looking at two further phonological issues, we should note one other morphological feature. This is that there are a very few verbs which have a reduced ablaut vowel in their present tense, and one of these verbs, namely *cuman* 'come', is of very high frequency. Such verbs are, for reasons we need not explore here, often called 'aorist presents'.

Turning to phonological issues, let me first discuss an issue which is not solely associated with strong verbs, but nevertheless is well represented there and can cause problems. This is the issue of contracted verbs. If you look back at the ablaut series, what you should be able to see is that in every class except classes III and IV it is possible for the stem of the verb to end in a voiceless velar fricative, i.e. /x/. In the development of this sound, which is usually spelled <h> as in (uncontroversially) a word such as *hēah* 'high' (see §1.7), this sound was weakened between vowels to the glottal fricative /h/ and then disappeared altogether.

In the cases that concern us the loss of /h/ means that there is no longer any consonant between the stem vowel and the inflection. Thus, if we take as an example the class V verb *sēon* 'see', this would at one stage have been *sīhan*. The loss of /h/ causes the stem vowel and the vowel of the inflection to merge together as a diphthong. If you know any German, then you might like to compare the present-day German form *sehen*. From our point of view, although these **contracted verbs**, as they are usually called, are somewhat awkward in much of their detail – with the result in Old English that some of them change their class membership quite readily – all we need note is that they are rather distinctive in that their infinitive form always ends *-ēon*, unlike any other verb except *bēon*, which has a similar source.

The second phonological issue is more complicated still, but is unavoidable. To see the problem, compare the paradigms of two class I verbs, *rīdan* 'ride' and *snīþan* 'cut':

rīdan	rād	ridon	-riden
snīþan	snāþ	snidon	-sniden

As can be seen, *snīþan* has an unexpected change in consonant in the past plural and past participle. This is a result of a Germanic sound change known as **Verner's Law**, after the nineteenth-century Danish linguist Karl Verner. What Verner discovered was that wherever a voiceless fricative occurred between voiced sounds, then that fricative became voiced provided that it was not preceded by the accent. After Verner's Law had operated, the stress patterns of the Germanic languages changed so, broadly speaking, stress always applied on the initial syllable. But previously the first syllables of past plural and past participles had been unstressed. Hence the alternations seen above.

Verner's Law predicts the following changes:

f → v; θ → ð; x → ɣ; s → z

However, mostly because of later sound changes, but also because of the Old English spelling system, the results of Verner's Law are frequently obscured. The easiest examples to follow are as in the paradigm of *snīþan*, where the only later alternation is that /ð/ has shifted to /d/, and the paradigm of *čēosan* (II), where /z/ becomes /r/:

| čēosan | čēas | curon | coren |

The alternation between *f* and *v* occurs in verbs such as *drīfan*, but it is obscured by the fact that the Old English spelling system does not use the symbol <v>. The examples showing the alternation between /x/ and /ɣ/ are shown, with /ɣ/ represented by <g> or with a sound change of /ɣ/ to /w/, <w>, but the examples involve contracted verbs, as you may have been able to deduce, so that we find, for example:

| sēon | seah | sāwon | sewen |

With the passage of time, almost all instances of Verner's Law have been lost from English, with the exception of the alternation *was ~ were* and occasional idiomatic expressions *lost and lorn*, where the first of the pair shows loss of Verner's Law, the second retention. Even in the Old English period there are clear signs that the alternation was on its way out. This is, for example, the case with the class I verb *rīsan* 'rise' which always has the paradigm:

| rīsan | rās | rison | risen |

Grammar books quite often give lists of verbs where Verner's Law has been lost. These lists are usually quite short, but there are two reasons why this happens. Firstly, in the very frequent case of verbs with medial *f*, as we have seen, it is simply orthographically impossible to obtain evidence one way or the other. Secondly, as everywhere else in Old

English, we can only work with the evidence we have. That is to say, if no text shows loss of Verner's Law in respect of a particular verb, all that this tells us is that there is no extant example of the loss, not that the loss never occurred. This is quite a subtle point, but the distinction is an important one, which should always be borne in mind when dealing with historical languages.

5.5 Modal verbs

As I said at the beginning of this chapter, the present-day English category of modals sits only uncomfortably into Old English. This is perhaps particularly true in terms of morphology. Historically speaking, the verbs which we call 'modals' almost all belonged to a group which is called **preterite-present** verbs. Such verbs originally had a preterite or past tense morphology but this morphology had acquired a present tense meaning. If we take a typical such verb, *cunnan* 'can, know', then it is possible to observe that it has many of the features which would be normally associated with a class III verb such as *singan*. In particular it can be observed that forms such as *cann* 'I know' and *cunnon* 'we know' relate in form to the past tense forms *sang* and *sungon* respectively. Even in present-day English we find *he can* and this lacks the final inflectional *-s* which we expect to find with every 3rd person singular verb; the lack of final *-s* is something that today we still associate only with strong verb past tense forms, as in *sang* 'he sang'.

Because these preterite-present verbs had forms which were preterite in form but present in meaning, they had to find new past forms from somewhere. The solution to this was to form a new past tense using the dental suffix associated with the weak verbs, although in a somewhat altered, and not always well understood, formation.

One obvious result of all this is that the preterite-present forms look rather irregular, both in their (new) present and past tense morphologies, and cannot easily be classified in a homogenous fashion. The other difficulty they present us with is the confusion which arises between morphological form and morphological content. Another way of putting this would be to describe this as the confusion between preterite-presents and modals, for the point is that not every preterite-present has modal features, and equally not every modal was a preterite-present verb. Add to this the fact that the modal category is not particularly robust in Old English, with some verbs showing modal syntactic features and others showing only semantic indications, and it is difficult to avoid the conclusion that the situation is a mess. It has to be said, however, that much of the mess is of our own devising, and reflects the results of attempting to use a nomenclature which can be shared between Old and present-day English. There is a judgement to be made about whether or not this is wise, and although the nomenclature does seem preferable, nevertheless a 'health warning' needs to be issued.

The above having been said, we can list the following modal verbs: *cann* 'know', *dearr* 'dare', *mæġ* 'be able', *mōt* 'can, must', *sċeal* 'must', *þearfan* 'need', *wile* 'want', but note that the last of these is not a preterite-present verb, although it shares many features with them. Note also that I have used as the citation form for these verbs the 3rd sing. present indicative rather than the infinitive. The reason for this is that two of these verbs, *mōt* and *sċeal*, do not appear to have had infinitive forms. The others did, but where they did, the infinitive has been lost whenever the verb is modal in present-day English. The absence of an infinitive is, therefore, one of the incipient developments of the modal category. Similarly, all these verbs, with the exception of *wile*, are without present and past participle forms, and here too the comparison with present-day English is instructive.

I give below, in a slightly summarised form, the paradigms of these verbs, from which it will be clear that there there are all somewhat irregular in comparison with most of the other verbs we have encountered. In these summaries I give only present tense singular and plural and the past tense 1 sing., since the other forms are easily derivable from those paradigms:

	cann	*dearr*	*mæġ*	*mōt*
1 Sing.	cann	dearr	mæġ	mōt
2 Sing.	canst	dearst	meaht	mōst
3 Sing.	cann	dearr	mæġ	mōt
Plural	cunnon	durron	magon	mōton
Subj. Sing.	cunne	durre	mæġe	mōte
Past	cūðe	dorste	meahte	mōste

	sċeal	*þearf*	*wile*
1 Sing.	sċeal	þearf	wille
2 Sing.	sċealt	þearft	wilt
3 Sing.	sċeal	þearf	wile
Plural	sċulon	þurfon	willað
Subj. Sing.	sċyle	þurfe	wille
Past	sċeolde	þorfte	wolde

Clearly there are some unexpected forms there, such as the presence of i-mutation in the present subjunctive of, say, *sċyle*, and its absence in *þurfe*, but in fact that is merely virtually free variation and exactly the opposite forms can also be found. Note also that many forms of *mæg*, especially in the past tense, are found with i-mutated variants, e.g. *mihte* alongside *meahte*. The infinitives, where they exist (see above), are as follows: *cunnan*, *durran*, *magan*, *þurfan*, *willan*.

There still remains to discuss the few preterite-presents which do not have any modal values. Perhaps the most frequent of these, although, as a whole, most of the group are relatively frequent, is *witan* 'know' with 3rd singular *wāt*. The basics of its paradigm are as follows:

1 Sing.	wāt
2 Sing.	wāst
3 Sing.	wāt
Plural	witon
Subj. Sing.	wite
Past	witað

Unlike most of the modals it has both a present and a past participle, namely *witende* and *ġewiten*. The other preterite-presents have paradigms similar to parallel modals. Hence *unnan* 'grant' is like *cunnan*; like *þurfan* is *ġemunan* 'remember'; *āgan* 'own', which might be included as a semi-modal, compare present-day English *ought*, and *dugan* 'avail' are parallel to *mōt*.

Exercises

The exercises in this chapter do not contain any text to translate, but instead I give two different exercises. The first of these is designed to help you to become familiar with strong verbs, since these undoubtedly form the most complex area of Old English morphology.

1. For each of the following verbs identify the strong verb class to which they belong and give their four principal parts: *helpan* 'help'; *brecan* 'break'; *brēotan* 'break'; *lūcan* 'lock'; *līðan* 'travel', *weorðan* 'become'; *slēan* 'slay'.

This chapter both marks the conclusion of detailed discussion of morphology, for in Chapter 6 I shall turn the discussion towards syntax, and it also marks the half-way point in the book. It is, therefore, a useful time to review the progress made so far. The following exercises are intended as one or two paragraph essays on the topics covered so far.

2. What are the principal features of Old English which distinguish it from that used today?

3. How many noun declensions were there in Old English? How many of these still exist, even if only minimally?

4. What are the principal differences between the different weak verb conjugations?

5. Examine in detail the variations possible within strong classes I–III.

6 Noun phrases and verb phrases

6.1 The elements of syntax

If you were to review some of the sample passages of Old English which I have presented in most of the exercises at the end of each chapter, it would, I think, become clear that Old English syntax presents a mixture of the old and the new. That is to say, although quite often the syntax of Old English sentences bears a close relationship to what is found today, there is also a good deal which is wholly unfamiliar. This, of course, is only to be expected, given that the two stages of the language are a thousand years or more apart. In what follows I attempt to concentrate on the 'old' rather than the 'new', but I hope that this can be done without losing sight of the latter.

Inevitably, given their concentration on morphology, the earlier chapters brought to the fore a number of issues which are substantially concerned with syntax. Examples of these include cases, adjective declension, and tense and mood. It therefore makes sense to start this part of the discussion with this type of issue before moving on in Chapter 7 to a discussion of sentence types and word order.

6.2 The noun phrase

The most basic syntactic elements in the noun phrase relate to case and number; gender, too, has a role in agreement phenomena. Since the biggest difference in these areas between Old and present-day English lies in the role of case, it is appropriate to start the discussion there.

Today nouns never show case inflection. Consider a sentence such as:

(1) The woman gave the man the book

and compare that with its Old English equivalent:

(2) þæt wīf ġeaf þǣm menn þā bōc

There, as can be seen by the three different forms of the demonstrative article, each noun phrase has a different case, nominative, accusative and dative. It might be thought that today there is one situation where there is nominal inflection:

(3) The woman's book

Compare to that:

(4) þæs wīfes bōc

I shall return to such Old English genitives later, but there is good reason for supposing that in the present-day language the *s* is no longer an inflection, but a **clitic** which is attached to an immediately-preceding noun phrase. If, therefore, I have to distinguish between the Old English construction and the present-day one, I shall do so by referring not to the Old English genitive but to the present-day possessive. The present-day possessive is, unlike the Old English genitive, not a case inflection, since it is not attached to a preceding noun, but rather to a whole noun phrase.

Now let's move on to the details of each case. The simplest order in which to take them is: nominative, accusative, dative and genitive. The nominative case is the case associated with the subject of a clause, and hence it is probably self-evident in its usage. Note that, since, unlike in Latin, there is no vocative case in Old English, the nominative is used for direct address:

(5) Lēofan men, ġecnāwaö þæt sōö is!
     dear   men   know   that truth is

As I shall discuss later, it is sometimes the case that there is no overt subject in Old English, but that is not something which concerns us immediately.

Just as the nominative is usually the sign of the subject, so too the most frequent, albeit not the only sign, of the direct object is the accusative case. Sometimes, despite the above, we find examples of a 'double accusative', that is to say, where there are two objects and both of them are in the accusative, but only one would be regarded as the direct object and the other an indirect object. Thus examples such as:

(6) An subdīacon bæd þone hālgan wer [IND OBJ] sumne dæl [OBJ] eles
     a subdeacon offered the holy man   some part of the oil

A further usage no longer found is the use of the accusative in expressions of the extent of place and time:

(7) Him wæs ealne weg [ACC] wēste land
     To him was all the way waste land

These constructions lead us on to another feature entirely absent from the present-day language. From a quite superficial, but traditional, point of view we can talk, in present-day English, about prepositions governing nouns, without at all thinking about what such **government** might mean. Once we begin to deal with an inflected language such as Old English, however, the meaning of government has to be elucidated.

We are, of course, entirely comfortable with the concept of verbs governing their objects. What has to be said now is that it is not only verbs which govern their objects; the same is also true of prepositions and their objects. This governance is realised by the case of the governed object. The majority of Old English prepositions required the dative case but a few usually required the accusative case, the most common of these being *ġeond* 'throughout', *þurh* 'through', *ymbe* 'about' and *oþ* 'until'. I keep using the adjective 'usually' because almost every preposition, whatever the usual case required may be, can govern the dative case as well, although this generally reflects a difference in meaning.

As distinct from the examples in the previous paragraph, which concern prepositions which are all fundamentally associated with the accusative case, there are a great many prepositions which can equally take either the accusative or the dative case. Such varied usage is common throughout the Indo-European family, and many present-day languages which retain a case system have also kept this prepositional usage. A nearby and obvious example is German. Now this varied usage is not random, but rather is based on meaning. When a preposition expresses motion in time and space it governs the accusative case, whereas when it expresses rest it governs the dative case. There are signs that this distinction is under threat, although it does not disappear until the case system itself is being lost.

The variations in prepositional usage which I have just discussed form only part of a more general feature of Old English government, which is probably more easily understood in the context of the dative case, to which I now turn. The use of the dative case which it is easiest for the modern reader to understand is to supply the function of the indirect object, as in the following:

(8) Geaf he & sealde þæt betste hors [ACC] ... Aidane þæm bisċeop [DAT]
    He gave and presented the best horse ... to Bishop Aidan

Until towards the end of the period prepositional *tō* is much less used, except with some verbs of, especially, saying, such as *cleopian*, *cweþan* and *sprecan*, where the indirect object is animate, as in:

(9) Hē cwæð tō mē
he said to me

Of course in present-day English there is a kind of survival of the dative in examples such as:

(10) She gave me it
(11) She gave the boy a present

but of course here it is position which indicates the indirect and direct objects.

There is a special use of the dative in Old English to express possession:

(12) ... þæt him þæt hēafod wand forð on ðā flōre
so that to him the head fell down to the floor

where the possessive pronoun has been replaced by *him* in the dative case. This can be compared with the French construction *à la main* 'in his hand'. It is, of course, true that the French construction is rather different. But in one crucial respect it is parallel, for it shows the use of a special construction: possession involving parts of the body. There are a number of other idiomatic constructions found quite frequently and which also use the dative case. These can often be viewed as fossilised idioms, and that is, for example, probably the best way of analysing the adverbial use of the dative in phrases such as *hwīlum* 'at times', *sume dæge*, *sumum dæge* 'one day'. The latter phrases occur alongside *on þisum dæge* with a preposition and hence double marking of the phrase.

The variation *sume dæge* ~ *sumum dæge* may be confusing for a moment, but it leads on to an important general point. When, in §3.3, I presented the indefinite declension of adjectives, I included an instrumental singular case. By the Old English period, although the instrumental case remains in use in some declensional paradigms, it is only vestigial and can be replaced by the dative, as in the variation I have just given. Nevertheless there are a few important instrumental constructions which should be noted. Above all, the use of the instrumental in expressions of cause is one that shows a clear inheritance in the present-day language. This occurs with both *hwȳ* 'why' and *þȳ* 'therefore':

(13) Hwȳ sēċe ġe ...
Why do you seek ...
(14) þȳ he cwæð nā ...
Therefore he said nothing ...

Hwȳ is, of course, the direct ancestor of the present-day *why*. These two forms are usually treated as part of the paradigms of, respectively, *se* 'that' and *hwā* 'who', and that is entirely reasonable, but their very particular usage may have meant that even in Old English they were becoming detached from their original paradigms.

A further instrumental usage which survives today, although not in a transparent fashion, is the type of idiom exemplified by *the more, the merrier*. Thus we find:

(15) Hiġe sċeal þe heardra ... þe ūre mæġen lytlað
      Courage will be *the* greater ... *the more* our strength lessens

Note that in this example from *The Battle of Maldon*, *þe*, which is usually classed as a particle, and to which I shall return in Chapter 7, appears as an alternative to *þȳ*, but is otherwise to be distinguished in this usage. A final use of the instrumental is one which is particular to Old English, and which, without any later development, is seen in a number of variations which together may be classed as partly manner and partly accompaniment. The former is seen in examples such as:

(16) sċolde here-byrne *hondum ġebroden*
      should be the war-corslet *hand woven*

and the latter in:

(17) Ond þā ġeascode hē þone cyning *lytle werode*
      And then he discovered the king *with a small group*

I have left aside until now one very significant use of the dative. In present-day English we are accustomed to analysing all direct objects identically, and therefore it might be assumed that in Old English this would simply surface as all direct objects being in the accusative case. That is indeed the norm. However there are many verbs which take a direct object in the dative rather than the accusative case. The following example shows this in practice:

(18) ... ðā kyningas ... Gode [DAT] ond his ǣrendwrecum [DAT] hīersumedon
          the kings ... God   and his messengers
      obeyed

There are too many verbs which take a dative object to permit a sensible listing of them here, although many of them will be found in the glossary. It is, however, worthy of note that some verbs take either an accusative object or a dative object, and that there may be a meaning distinction available, as in these two sentences which show different meanings of *folgian*:

(19) ond ðā folgode feorhġeniðhlan [ACC]
      then (he) pursued deadly foes
(20) him [DAT] folgiaþ fuglas [NOM]
      him   followed birds 'birds followed him'

Moving now to the genitive, perhaps the first point to make is that the syntax of the genitive case is in most respects rather similar to that of the possessive in present-day English. The second point to make, on the other hand, marks a distinction between Old English and present-day English, and to clarify this it is useful to distinguish between the Old English genitive and the present-day possessive. For both the genitive and the possessive we can characterise their prototypical function as being to mark a relationship between two nouns. Thus in both (21) and (22):

(21) ... tō þæs cyninges [GEN] untruman bearne [DAT]
(22) ... to the king's sickly child

the crucial feature is that there is a functional relationship between *cyninges/king's* and *bearn/child*, and that relationship is the same at both stages of the language. But what are not found in Old English are phrases such as the following present-day construction:

(23) The woman down the street's cat

where the possessive marker is not found on the possessing noun (*woman*), but rather on phrase-final noun (*street*). That is to say, it is the woman who possesses the cat (if anyone can ever be said to possess a cat!), not the street. The possessive marker, therefore, is attached, not to the noun which enters the possessive relationship, but rather to the final noun of the phrase. Therefore there is a significant difference here between the two stages of the language.

Having dealt with that matter, it's now possible to look in more detail at the functions of the Old English genitive case. The principal uses of the genitive, as I have indicated, are to show the functional relationships between two nouns, thus we can talk of subjective genitives, where the noun in the genitive acts as the subject of the second noun. Such uses are very common, and can be exemplified by examples such as:

(24) þæs bisċeopes bodung

where the bishop is doing the preaching, i.e. the bishop is the subject of the preaching.

The obvious opposite of this is the objective genitive, as in *folces weard* 'the guardian of the people'. However, as in present-day English it can be difficult to tell whether the genitive is being used subjectively or objectively, to the point of complete ambiguity. Thus the phrase *godes lufu* is, at least out of context, ambiguous, since it could mean either 'the love God has (for someone)', or 'the love someone has for God'. Of course, exactly the same holds for present-day English. Other types of genitive include the descriptive genitive found in, for example:

(25) Se wæs mæres līfes man
'he was a man of famous life'

and the partitive genitive, as in *ān heora* 'one of them'. It is possible, although not necessarily fruitful, to further subdivide the categories above, but that can make it difficult to see the general principles behind the use of the genitive.

This is especially important here, because, in addition to the above uses which closely resemble those in present-day English, there are a few types of genitive which no longer exist or do so only in an altered form. One such example is the genitive of measure, as in *fīf nihta first* 'a five nights' period', where present-day constructions usually prefer an *of*-construction, thus 'a period of five nights'. A rather common usage is the adverbial usage of the genitive, best exemplified in the phrase *dæges and nihtes* 'by day and by night', also found alone, i.e. *dæges* 'by day', *nihtes* 'at night'. Note that *nihtes* has the inflection appropriate to masculine nouns in this construction, rather than the usual *nihte*, which rather implies a stereotyped idiom. You might also like to compare the present-day construction *he works nights*. Note also the use of the genitive form of demonstrative *þæs*, which has the meaning 'therefore, so'.

As with the dative case, a number of verbs normally or often take a genitive object. The situation here is often quite parallel to the use of the dative. Although it is possible to give some indication of what kinds of verb have a genitive direct object, for example verbs of depriving and also of rejoicing, e.g. *blissian* 'rejoice', such guides are far from infallible; it is also worth noting that verbs taking a genitive object may also often take the accusative, and that can be dependent on whether the object is abstract [GEN] or animate [ACC]. As in cases involving the dative, I have attempted to note the case usage in the glossary.

There are few prepositions which regularly take the genitive case. The only common examples are *andlang* 'along', *tō* 'to', especially in expressions of time; note particularly the use of *tō* + genitive in the phrase *tō þæs þe* 'until', and *wiþ* when it means 'towards' rather than 'against'.

6.3 Concord

We are used to **agreement** or **concord** in present-day English between a subject and its verb, as seen in the difference between the two sentences below:

(26) The **cat is** sleeping on the mat

(27) The **cats are** sleeping on the mat

Other than this, rather restricted example, grammatical agreement is non-existent in English today. But in Old English there is not only concord between subject and verb, but also between the elements within a noun phrase, that is to say, demonstratives, adjectives and nouns, between pronouns and the items to which they refer, and between pronouns and modifiers of those pronouns. Since so much of Old English concord takes place in the noun phrase, I have chosen to deal with all the principal effects of concord here, all in one place.

Subject-verb agreement essentially works in much the same way in Old English as in present-day English. That is to say, its basis is that the subject noun agrees in number and person with the verb. Thus we find:

(28) Se kāsere [SING] hine underfēng [SING] ... and þā romaniscan witan [PL] hine wurðodon [PL] swyðe
The emperor welcomed him ... and the Roman senators honoured him greatly

The kinds of exceptions to subject-verb concord are not dissimilar to exceptions which sometimes occur in present-day English. Thus when two singular nouns form a compound subject, then the verb is often singular, as in:

(29) þær sċeal [SING] bēon ġedrync and pleġa
there will be drinking and playing

Such agreement is most frequent when, as in (29), the verb precedes its subject. A different type occurs with *hit* 'it', *þæt* 'that' and *hwæt* 'who, what', which frequently have a plural verb and complement, as in:

(30) þæt [SING] sindon ūre synna
that are our sins

As in present-day English, so in Old English, there could be a conflict between grammatical concord and semantic concord. This can be seen both in examples with indefinite pronouns, as in (31), and in examples with a collective noun, as in (32):

(31) þonne rīdeð [SING] ælc, and hit motan [PL] habban
then each one rides, and can have it

(32) sēo buruhwaru [SING] hine underfēngon [PL]
the township received him

The second example is like the variation found particularly in British English between *the committee is* and *the committee are*.

Turning now to concord in the noun phrase, the first point to note is that demonstratives and adjectives agree in number, case and gender with their head noun. That this does not, for the most part, happen in present-day English is simply due to the loss of inflections which has taken place. Some demonstratives, of course, do still show number, hence *this* ~ *these*. The principle therefore remains. Furthermore, of course, other present-day languages such as German and French do show, to some degree, agreement between adjectives and their nouns.

The essential rule in Old English is just as explained above, namely that demonstratives and adjectives agree with their head noun. Thus we find, for example:

(33) þæs heofonlican līfes [GEN SING NEUT]
of the heavenly life
(34) þā ġelǣredestan men [ACC PL MASC]
the most learned men

It should be noted, of course, that the same rules of agreement apply regardless of whether an adjective is definite, as in (33–34), or indefinite, as in (35):

(35) (hē wæs) līchomliċre untrymnesse þryċċed [DAT SING FEM]
(he was) with bodily weakness oppressed

and the agreement is entirely distinct from the syntactically-motivated choice of adjective declension.

Although agreement is quite strictly observed in Old English, there are some situations where complete agreement is impossible. The most obvious cases involve two nouns of different gender but which share a common adjective, as in:

(36) wit [i.e. Adam and Eve] hēr baru [NOM PL NEUT] standað
we stand here naked

As can be seen, the adjective is in the neuter gender, even though the nouns to which it refers back are, respectively, masculine and feminine. A further feature, which is far more often found in later texts, is the simplification of plural adjective forms in a single common gender which is the historical masculine gender, as can be found in other languages too, for example Italian. Although this will not cause difficulty, it should be noted as a sign of the simplification which will become standard in later centuries.

Despite the comments above, it should be noted that the normal situation in Old English is to preserve gender agreement. This is best seen in the agreement of pronouns and their antecedents.

(37) ... swyðe miċel sǣ [FEM] up in on lande, sēo [FEM] is brādre þonne ǣniġ mann ofer sēon mæġe
a very large sea inland, she is wider than any man can see over.

Yet when there is a disagreement between grammatical gender and natural gender, then the pronoun can show natural rather than grammatical gender:

(38) Sum wīf [NEUT] hātte Sintiċe, sēo [FEM] wæs blind ...
A certain woman called Syntyche, she was blind ...

6.4 Tense in the verb phrase

I have already, in earlier chapters, discussed the fact that in Old English there were only two tenses, namely present and past. If this fact is kept in mind, then some potential difficulties can be easily avoided. However, there are a number of points to note in this basic proposition. Firstly, future time is regularly expressed by the present tense:

(39) iċ arīse and iċ fare tō mīnum fæder
I shall arise and go to my father

It is noteworthy that neither *willan* 'will' nor *sċeal* 'shall' have the meaning of futurity as they do in present-day English, except in the occasional, and rather literal, translation of a Latin future. The following example from Ælfric is not strictly a translation, but it certainly reflects the Latin original:

(40) þā dēadan sċeolon arīsan
the dead shall arise again

Of course this example can also express, just as the present-day modal does, necessity with future implication.

Yet in reported speech we find examples which do not look as if they are a copy of Latin and in which *sċeolde* 'should' represents a future in the past:

(41) Hīe ne wēndon ðætte ǣfre menn sċeolden swǣ reccelēase weorðan
They did not think that ever men would so reckless become

6.5 Aspect

As well as expressing time relationships by means of tense, Old English also expressed such relationships by means of aspect, a grammatical feature which in English is used to present, not the time of an action, but rather how the action took place. In present-day English there are usually said to be two aspects, one realised by *have* + *past participle*, e.g. *I have seen*, one realised by *be* + *present participle*, e.g. *I was dreaming*. There is often much argument about the appropriate labels to attach to these constructions; here I shall refer to the former as perfective aspect, but I shall refer to the latter merely as *be+ing*, since there is no ready equivalence between Old English and present-day English constructions.

Although there are significant differences of both form and meaning between perfective aspect in Old English and present-day English, the construction we find today is clearly a development of that pertaining in Old English. Thus the following sentence parallels its modern counterpart:

(42) Maria hæfð ġecoren þæt betste dæl
      Mary has chosen the best part

There is one significant difference between the two stages of the language, and at the same time we have to bear in mind the frequent use in Old English of the simple past in constructions where we would prefer the perfect or even the past perfect.

The difference I have in mind is that in Old English the perfective was expressed by two constructions, the choice of which was determined by the verb type. As in (42), one construction was formed by *habban* + *past participle*, the other by *bēon* + *past participle*, as can be seen in (43):

(43) Hīe wǣron cumen Lēoniðan tō fultume
      They had come to help Leonidas

This variation in construction is one that will be familiar to anyone who knows a language such as German, and it is based on the same principles, namely that transitive verbs form the perfect with *habban* and intransitive verbs use *bēon*.

The perfective aspect seems to have had its origin in a construction where *habban* had a full lexical, rather than grammatical, usage, with a normal object, as in present-day:

(44) She has those letters

to which, as it were, a post-modifying participial adjective is attached, giving a structure such as:

(45) *She has those letters found

There is good evidence that this was a development underway during the Old English period. A particularly good example is the following from Ælfric:

(46) Fela Godes wundra wē habbað ġehyred [UNINFLECTED] and ēac ġeswene [ACC PL]
Many wonders we have heard and also seen

In this sentence with a compound participial structure, the first participle *ġehȳred* is uninflected, corresponding to the type *She has found those letters* in present-day English, whilst the second participle is inflected, like the type in (45). This variation between inflected and uninflected forms can be seen as one sign of adjectival usage shifting to verbal morphology. In Old English the majority of forms are already uninflected and this proportion seems to increase with the passage of time. The intransitive forms with *bēon* are largely parallel to the transitive forms, except that the inflected participle is in the nominative, which is predictable, and usually shows -Ø in the singular and -e in the plural. Thus we find examples such as:

(47) hū sīo lār lædenġeðīodes ær ðissum afeallen wæs
how the teaching of Latin by then had fallen away

Another example from the same text, Alfred's *Cura Pastoralis*, exemplifies a much less common use of the feminine inflection:

(48) Swæ clæne hīo [FEM] wæs oðfeallenu
so completely it was fallen away

It should be noted here that the presence or absence of inflection is not the only, nor even necessarily safe, proof of the shift to verbal structure. As I shall discuss in Chapter 7, another issue here is word order.

The rivalry between *habban* and *bēon* which has eventually led to the virtually complete loss of the latter type in present-day English was already apparent in Old English. Thus it is possible to find examples such as:

(49) þā Scipia hæfde ġefaren tō ðære nīwan byriġ Cartaina
Then Scipio had travelled to the new city of Carthage

Turning now to the use of *bēon* + *present participle*, there is no doubt that the construction was used in Old English, sometimes quite frequently. But if we look at the following two examples:

(50) eall middanġeard bið þonne on dæġ byrnende
all the earth is then by day burning

(51) hit God siþþan longsumliċe wrecende wæs
      it God afterwards for a long time avenging was

it should be clear that there are significant differences between the Old English and present-day structures, for in (51) we use a simple past tense today, i.e. *God avenged it* ... There are other examples too where the Old English construction cannot be easily moulded into the present-day one:

(52) Ond hīe þā ymb þā gatu feohtende wæron oþ þæt hīe þærinne fulgon
      And they then around the gates fighting were until they therein burst

where the sense of the construction is 'continued fighting until ...'.

It is also clear that the simple present tense was often used for expressions where present-day English would use *be + present participle*:

(53) ðēos worold is on ofste and hit nēalæcð þām ende
      this world is in haste and it is approaching its end

A further alternative in past tense environments was to use *wolde*, the past tense form of *willan*, in order to show habitual aspect, one of the features of the present-day *be + present participle* construction:

(54) Hē wolde æfter ūhtsange oftost hine ġebiddan
      He would, after matins, regularly pray

In summary, there are links between the Old English and present-day constructions, but there are also substantial differences, which preclude any real sense of identity.

6.6 Voice

With one exception, which I discuss below, Old English had no morphological passive. Instead, much as in the present-day language, the passive was often expressed periphrastically. Today the construction is *be + past participle*, and the Old English equivalent is *bēon + past participle*. Thus we find many examples like:

(55) Æfter þæm þe Romeburg ġetimbred wæs
      After Rome had been built

But there is an interesting alternative construction in which the verb is not *bēon* but rather *weorþan* 'become', everything else remaining unchanged. Thus we find examples such as:

(56) þæt hūs wearð ðā forburnen
      the house was then burnt down

There has been much effort expended on the distinction in meaning between the two alternatives. There is some agreement that quite often, but not categorically, *bēon* is used in stative contexts and *weorðan* in dynamic contexts, and that variation is discernible in the differences in meaning between (55) and (56). However, it is best viewed as a tendency rather than as a rule occasionally violated. Some Old English writers seem to have made more use of the distinction than others.

The above variation can seem confusing, since, of course, it has been lost from the language since the Old English period, and we no longer have the verb *weorðan*. Two points can be made here. Firstly, it is worth, if possible, looking at either Dutch or German, for both these languages have retained the equivalent of *weorþan* (Dutch *worden*, German *werden*, albeit with different uses) and they both have a clear distinction between the uses of that verb and of the equivalent of *bēon*. Secondly, it is worth considering in this context the uses of present-day English *get* (similar to Dutch *worden* but not German *werden*), as in:

(57) She got fired by her boss

Another aspect of *weorþan*, and one I ignored earlier, is that it can also replace *bēon* in the other periphrastic constructions we have looked at in this section. I did not discuss those examples earlier because they are much less frequent than this use in the passive. You should, however, be aware that they are possible.

Rather than using the periphrastic passive, Old English, again like Dutch and German, could use *man* 'one', as in:

(58) mon mæġ ġīet ġesīon hiora swæð
      one could still see their track

Note that this usage, although reminiscent of present-day *one*, did not have any of the social connotations often associated with *one*. The use of *man* was perfectly normal and very frequent.

Despite the above, there did exist in Old English one morphological passive, namely *hātte*, *hatton*, passive forms of hātan 'call'. Typical examples of this frequent form are:

(59) His fæder hātte Gordianus
      His father was called Gordianus
(60) ... under twǣm consulum, Tīta and Publia hātton
      under two consuls, called Tita and Publia

On the other hand, at least as frequent is the periphrastic structure as in:

(61) and þes dēofol þe is ġehaten antechrist
      and this devil is called the antichrist

It is probably foolish to attach too much importance to this morphological passive. It looks rather like a idiomatic relic.

6.7 Mood

The default mood in Old English, as in present-day English, was the indicative mood. In other words, Old English verbs used the indicative paradigm unless there was some reason for using an alternative mood. It is useful to describe the use of the indicative in terms of an 'elsewhere' condition, i.e. everywhere where there is no other specific requirement. Apart from the fact that this makes the discussion here easier, it also reflects the later development of the language.

The mood which is regularly opposed to the indicative is the subjunctive mood. For present-day speakers of English, who may not even be aware that there still remains, albeit somewhat vestigially, a subjunctive mood, the subjunctive can be confusing; this is not so true for those who know languages such as French and German, where the subjunctive remains salient.

It is possible to list a large number of ways in which the subjunctive is used in Old English, but it is more important to understand the general principles which govern its usage. And these may be collected together under one such principle, namely that the subjunctive is used when the speaker does not wish to vouch for the factual status of what is being said. Note that this is not the same as when a speaker claims that something is false.

It happens that one of the few remaining uses of the subjunctive in present-day English helps to show how this works. In:

(62) If I were [SUBJ] you (which I'm not!) I would study astrology
      instead

the subjunctive is used because the statement made in that clause is plainly false. Of course, in Old English, as in other languages with the subjunctive, this massively simplifies the situation. The speaker expresses his or her belief simply by his or her use of the subjunctive rather than the indicative.

One common use of the Old English subjunctive is in clauses of condition:

(63) sēċ, ġif þū dyrre!
      seek if you dare!

but note that (63), unlike (62), is not counterfactual. An obviously similar type occurs with clauses of concession:

(64) þēah man swā ne wēne
    although they don't think so

One rather notable use of the subjunctive occurs in reported speech, where it is used to indicate that the truth of the reported claim is not guaranteed. It is important to remember that this is not at all the same as saying that the claim is false. The following long example is rather interesting (I have italicised the three critical verb forms):

(65) Wulfstān sǣde þæt hē *gefōre* of Hǣðum, þæt hē *wǣre* on Trūsō on in syfan dagum and nihtum, þæt þæt sċip *wæs* ealne weġ yrnende under seġle
    Wulfstan said that he went from Hedeby, that he was in Druznyo seven days and nights, that the ship was all the way running under sail

The use of the subjunctive here merely indicates that this is what Wulfstan said and does not imply disbelief. But note also that the final critical verb form is in the indicative. That is due to a process of distance concord; at that point the distance between the subject (*Wulfstan*) and the verb is so great that the grammatical agreement has been lost sight of.

Two other uses of the subjunctive are of general interest. Firstly it can be used to express a wish, as in:

(66) God ūre helpe!
    God help us!

As the translation shows, this usage remains in present-day English; compare *God helps us*. The second use is after verbs expressing doubt or possibility, as can be seen in the following example:

(67) For ðy iċ wolde ðætte hīe ealneg æt ðǣre stōwe wǣren [SUB]
    Therefore I would like that it always at the place were

The particular interest of this type, of course, is that it parallels constructions found in present-day languages such as French, Italian and German. It would be possible to extend the discussion of the subjunctive considerably, but I am not convinced that that would be helpful at this stage. It is perhaps more important for you to recognise subjunctives when you find them and then attempt yourself to explain why they occur, given the principles above. But even in Old English, the similarity of indicative and subjunctive inflection resulted in many cases where it has become uncertain whether an indicative or an subjunctive was intended. Later, this is going to promote the loss of a distinctive subjunctive in a great many instances.

In the chapters on morphology I indicated that there were distinctive forms for the imperative singular and plural, and these are, I think self-explanatory. In addition, however, there is a special imperative form for the 1st person plural, namely *uton*, which is very similar to present-day English *let's* in its use, as can be seen from an example such as:

(68) Utan faran to Bethleem
      let's travel to Bethlehem

For third person exhortations, the subjunctive is used, as can also happen today, as the gloss to (67), discussed above, shows. With a small number of verbs roughly equivalent to the modal verbs in present-day English, the infinitive can directly follow, as in:

(69) Hwæt sċeal iċ singan?
      what must I sing?

A use of the infinitive which has been quite lost from English is its use with verbs of rest or motion, as in:

(70) Hē ēode eft sittan siððan mid his ðegnum
      He went again [to] sit then with his disciples

So far I have completely ignored one morphological form of the infinitive. You may also have wondered about the Old English correspondent to the familiar *to*-infinitive of present-day English. The two points are connected. As well as the usual infinitive forms we have observed, there was a further infinitive form, so that we find forms such as *fremmenne* or *fremmanne* and *lufienne* or *lufianne*, corresponding to the plain infinitives *fremman, lufian*. These are traditionally called **inflected infinitives**, and the important point to note is that they always occur with the preposition *tō*. Thus we find:

(71) ... þæt þe is riht tō habbenne
      that this is right to have

The *tō* + *inflected infinitive* construction is very common, and it is used to express meanings of, for example, necessity, purpose and completion. It can also be used as either the subject or the complement of a clause. Because of your knowledge of present-day English, the examples you will come across will stand out and will not cause you any great difficulty.

Exercise

In this exercise I present you, for the first time, with a reasonably self-contained piece of Old English, and I no longer give you any help with glossing. You should, instead, use the glossary at the end of the book. The extract I have chosen is one of the most famous texts in Old English, namely the *Sermo Lupi ad Anglos*, written in 1014 by Wulfstan, Archbishop of York. At this time the question of whether Anglo-Saxon England was to be ruled by English kings or by Danish kings was critical to the country, and, as we know, Cnut (Canute) was indeed shortly to gain power.

The full text shows the power of Wulfstan's rhetoric, but even the extract I present here, from the start of the sermon, is impressive in itself. You might like to imagine yourself as an Anglo-Saxon listening to even the very first sentence. Many of Wulfstan's rhetorical devices are an echo of the poetic forms of the time, and I shall return to that in Chapter 9.

Lēofan men, ġecnāwað þæt sōð is: ðēos worold is on ofste, and hit nēalæcð þām ende; and þy hit is on worolde, aa swā leng, swā wyrse, and swā hit sċeal nyde for folċes synnan ǣr Antecrīstes tōcyme yfelian swyþe; and hūru hit wyrð þænne eġeslić and grimlić wīde on worolde. Understandað ēac ġeorne þæt dēofol þās þēode nū fela ġēara dwelode tō swyþe, and þæt lytle ġetrēowþa wǣran mid mannum, þēah hy wel spǣcan, and unrihta tō fela ricsode on lande; and næs ā fela manna þe smēade ymbe þā bōte swā ġeorne swā man sċolde, ac dæġhwāmlīċe man īhte yfel æfter ōðrum and unriht rǣrde and unlaga maneġe ealles tō wīde ġynd ealle þās þēode.

7 Clauses

7.1 Word order

One of the most obvious contrasts between Old English and present-day English is word order. This term, however, can be approached from many different angles, such as, on the one hand, the order in which the subject, verb and object or complement are found and, on the other, the order in which modifiers of the noun are presented. These various word orders are often inter-related, as I shall occasionally discuss in the course of this chapter.

However, it is probably best to start with the most salient of these features, namely subject-verb-object word order, in other words the relative placing of the principal phrases within any clause. Within this topic the best place to start is with present-day English. There we find what is sometimes described as fixed word order. That is to say, there appears to be a prescribed sequence such that the subject precedes the verb which in turn precedes the object (if there is one). Thus:

(1) The dog [SUBJ] bit [VERB] the man [OBJ]

Such a structure will seem obvious to the point of tedium. But there are exceptions. One type of exception is, crudely speaking, stylistic. Here, for example, we find examples such as (2):

(2) Cheese [OBJ] I like, tomatoes [OBJ] I hate

where the two objects of the two clauses have been placed in front of their subjects and verbs in order to achieve a special effect. That type of stylistic device is available in Old English too. But there is also another type of exception, which can be seen in:

(3) Along came [VERB] Jones [SUBJ].

This is not a matter of stylistics; rather it is alternative structural (as opposed to stylistic) word order. It may be uncommon, but for our purposes the most important point is that it exists.

The dominance of one fixed word order in present-day English can invite monolingual speakers of the language, or those who only know French or Spanish in addition, to assume that this is the normal situation amongst the languages of the world. Indeed, what we can call for the moment SVO word order is very common. Other languages have, however, different orders. Welsh, for example, has VSO word order, so not even in Britain do all the languages share the same word order.

What does all this have to do with Old English? If we turn (1) above into Old English, it would be something like:

(4) Se docga bāt þone guman

Clearly the word order is the same as in present-day English. And it is true that structures like this are commonplace in Old English. However, it is not the only possible type of order. In terms of basic word order Old English reflects a changing pattern which, as (3) above in one respect demonstrates, has never been completely stabilised.

It appears that in Old English there were two competing word orders: there was an SVO order as in the present-day language, but there was also an SOV word order, as occurs, for example, in Latin. This may seem confusing, but similar facts hold, albeit in somewhat different ways, in present-day Germanic languages such as German and Dutch. This should, by now, be a familiar feature, namely that Old English often looks as much like German or Dutch as English. It is a recurring pattern and simply emphasises the Germanic origins of English.

7.2 Verb-second order

However, rather than talking about SVO and SOV word order, it is rather more enlightening, I think, to talk of **verb-second** and **verb-final** word order. In other words, the critical point is whether the verb comes second or last in its clause. I shall start to explain what this means immediately, but if you look back at (4) you will see that the verb *bāt* does indeed come second in its clause, with the subject noun phrase in first position.

This helps us to understand what verb-second means: it means that the verb is placed after the first important element in the clause. In present-day English this first element has become virtually equated with the subject, hence the identity of (1) and (4). But there was no such equation in Old English. The question arises, therefore, of what a first element might be if it can be something other than a subject. Probably the most frequent cases involve an adverbial. Thus the following is usual:

(5) þā becōm hē tō Westseaxan
Then came he to the West Saxons

But the modern order can also be found:

(6) Oswold þā arǣrde āne rōde
Oswald then erected a cross

Such variation can be confusing, but it arises out of two related features. Firstly, the modern order may have been chosen in examples like (6) for reasons of text structure, here to focus attention on the fact that Oswald did something. Secondly, the older word order is beginning to be lost, a process which will accelerate during the early Middle English period. The two features may well have interacted.

þā is by no means the only adverbial which acts in this way, and, furthermore, the same word order is also frequently seen with adverbial phrases:

(7) On þām ylċan tīman cōm ēac sum bisċeop fram Rōmebyriġ
At the same time came also a bishop from Rome

Here too it is probable that the adverbial phrase is the first element in order to express the discourse feature of **focus**.

þā is extremely frequent, but there is another adverbial of similar frequency which both displays verb-second order and is also very important indeed. This is *ne* 'not', the principal means for expressing negation. This too prefers verb-second word order, as in:

(8) Ne cōm se here
Not came the army

but since I want to look at negation later in this chapter I shall forego further discussion here. In questions, too, the verb occupies second position after an interrogative pronoun:

(9) Hwæt eart þū?
Who are you?

but the same also happens even when there is no interrogative:

(10) Gehyrst þū, sǣlida, hwæt þis folc seġeð?
Hearest thou, sailor, what these people say?

The similarity of this construction to that in present-day English is only obscured by the use of the dummy auxiliary verb *do* which is now regular:

(11) Do you hear, sailor, what these people are saying?

It is worth noting as more than an aside that Old English never had such a dummy auxiliary verb. The similarities between the Old English and present-day English constructions can be very clearly seen in examples involving modal auxiliaries. Compare, therefore, the following pair:

(12) Canst þū temian hīġ?
(13) Can you tame them?

All the above examples share the characteristic that the first element in the clause is something other than a subject noun phrase, but the most usual situation is in (4), where the first element is the subject. Typical examples are the following:

(14) Se messeprēost leofode be hlāfe and be wætere
      The mass-priest lived on bread and water
(15) Drihten sǣde þis biġspel his leorningcnihtum
      The Lord told this story to his disciples

which are clearly parallel to present-day structures.

One structure which shows an overt verb-subject structure but which is quite different from the interrogative structure shown in (11) is exemplified by many sentences of type in (16):

(16) Wæs hē se mon in weoruldhāde ġeseted ...
      was he a man settled in the secular life ...

Such sentences have a presentative structure, which is rather similar to the present-day structure seen in sentences such as:

(17) There rose in his imagination grand visions of a world empire

Compare with (17):

(18) Grand visions of a world empire rose in his imagination

The flexibility accorded to Old English by means of the role of inflections makes the possibility of presentative structures less clumsy there than they are today.

As I move towards a discussion of verb-final word order, we need firstly to look at a structure which, on the surface, appears to show verb-final word order. It can be exemplified by (19):

(19) Ond hēo [SUBJ] hine [OBJ] þā monade [VERB]
      And she him then encouraged

This is, however, in fact a verb-second construction, even although the verb comes after not merely the subject, but also the object. Let me now explain how this might be so, contrary to immediate impressions.

The explanation for this leads us to a further distinctive feature of Old English. This is that there is a distinction made which concerns the **weight** of syntactic phrases. There was a clear preference in Old English to place light elements, that is to say, elements with only minimal phonological content, towards the beginning of clauses, and, conversely, to place elements with a great deal of phonological content at the end of clauses. And the placement of object pronouns before their verbs, as in (19), is the clearest example of this weight principle. You may find it useful to compare this type of construction with the placement of object pronouns with the same placement that occurs in a language such as French, for example *Il les aime*, which corresponds to English *He likes them.*

It is important to note that when the clause has a first element other than a subject, then an object pronoun will still precede the verb, provided that the subject is not a pronoun itself. Thus we find:

(20) Fela spella [ACC] him [DAT] sǣdon þā Beormas [NOM]
      Many stories to him told the *Beormas*

but if the subject is also a pronoun and there is a non-subject first element, then both pronouns follow the verb:

(21) þā sǣde he [SUBJ] him [DAT] þis biġspel [ACC]
      then told he them this story

The interaction of weight features and the, as it were, 'ordinary' word order is complex, or certainly seems so to anyone, such as a speaker of present-day English, whose own language pays much less attention to weight.

7.3 Verb-final order

It might be thought that given all the variations I have already discussed, you would be forgiven for thinking that verb-final order was relatively insignificant in Old English. Far from it! It is, indeed, very common, and historically, too, it is very important. The reason for its historical importance is that, as far as we can judge, verb-final order is much older than verb-second order. This is an issue I touched upon towards the end of §7.1, and it is worth emphasising here.

If at some pre-historical time the ancestor of Old English, and the other Germanic languages, had been regularly verb-final, then what we are seeing during the Old English period is a gradual, and incomplete, shift away from that and towards verb-second. There is neither space nor time to elaborate on this here, but one point we might note is when such a change occurs, it seems to affect main clauses before subordinate clauses. That certainly happens in Old English. But the prototypical locus of verb-final order is in subordinate clauses, which is exactly what we could predict, given what I have just said.

So, if we take the following example which is merely the continuation of (19) above, you should be able to see that in the subordinate noun clause (italicised for convenience) the verb appears finally after both the subject and the object:

(22) ond hēo hine þā monade ond lǣrde *þæt hē* [NOM] *woruldhād* [OBJ] *ānforlēte* [VERB]
  and she him then encouraged and taught *that he secular life should forsake*

There is some variation in the usage of verb-final order in subordinate clauses, and at least in part this seems to have been a matter of discourse. Thus relative clauses clearly prefer verb-final order, as in:

(23) ... sumne dǣl þæs mēoses *þe hēo mid beweaxen wæs*
  ... a part of the moss *with which it overgrown was*

as do clauses of time, as in:

(24) Sende ðā to Scotlande, *þǣr se ġelēafa wæs ðā*
  sent then to Scotland, *where the faith was then*

But despite (22) above, noun clauses quite often show verb-second position.

It would be wrong to give the impression that verb-final position is only found in subordinate clauses, even if that is the prototypical position for that word order. In main clauses there is also the possibility of finding what looks at first sight like a strange mixture of verb-second and verb-final orders. Consider the following example:

(25) ... hū sīo ǣ *wæs* ǣrest on Ebrisċġeðīode *funden*
  ... how the law was first in Hebrew found

Note that the two verbs in the complex verb phrase have been separated, so that the first part appears in verb-second position and the second part appears in verb-final position.

The only possible explanation of structures such as this is that we are witnessing part of the process of change from a verb-final to a verb-second word order, in which only the first verb in the verb phrase is permitted to occupy the new verb-second position, with any remaining verb remaining in verb-final position. But at a time where the two basic word order patterns are clearly rivals, it is not surprising that we find alternative structures:

(26) Nū *habbaþ* ḡē *ḡehyred* þā Hālgan þrȳnesse
      Now have you heard the Holy Trinity

where the verbs are not separated, except by the light personal pronoun. In subordinate clauses where we expect to find verb-final order in any case, the complex verb is not separated. The following example shows more than merely that:

(27) þā hī *eten hæfdon*, hī wunedon ðǣr
      When they eaten had, they stayed there

for you will be able to see that the order of the two verbs is the opposite of what you might have expected. If you have some knowledge of present-day German the constructions I have just mentioned may be somewhat familiar to you. And if you know any Dutch, that is even better, for Dutch has some, although not all, of the variations I have mentioned.

It would be possible to spend more time on the above word order issues, for I have only scratched the surface, and in particular I have not really explored the many variations which arise in real text. However, in order to demonstrate at least some of the complexities which arise it is worth taking a quick look at one example of the kind of thing which actually occurs. Look, therefore, at the following main clause:

(28) þā Scipia hæfde ḡefaren tō ðǣre nīwan byriḡ Cartaina
      Then Scipio had travelled to the new city (of) Carthage

There are two problems here. Firstly, since this is recognisably a main clause, the first part of the verb ought to occupy verb-second position, immediately after *þā*; secondly, the second part of the verb ought to occupy final position in the clause. Why are both verbs in the 'wrong' place? In the case of *hæfde* the reason is probably a matter of discourse structure. If the sentence has started *þā hæfde Scipia* ... it would appear as if part of a list, as in present-day English *Then ... then ... then ...* But the actual context of the sentence (trust me on this one!) shows that this sentence starts a new, or resumed, topic and therefore *Scipia* is promoted to second place over *hæfde*. In the case of *ḡefaren* the problem arises because the following phrase is heavy, and therefore the principle that heavy elements should appear as near as possible to the end of the clause comes into play.

7.4 Noun phrase order

Most of the word order properties associated with the internal structure of noun phrases are quite similar to those found in present-day English. After the complexities of clause word order, this may come to you as a relief. Indeed, it is fair to claim that the most difficult issue of all is one that we have already dealt with, namely the double declension of adjectives, according to whether they are definite or indefinite, see §3.3. I shall therefore principally discuss only a few issues where differences between Old English and present-day English are either clear or significant.

In general, elements have an order which is readily apparent, so that there is a general sequence of *demonstrative* + *adjective* + *noun*. If there is a possessive present, as in present-day English, it occupies the demonstrative slot. It should be noted that *eall* 'all' usually precedes all other items in the noun phrase, as, of course, it does in present-day English. And, of course, no demonstrative has quite the same function in Old English as the definite article has in present-day English. Equally, but more emphatically still, there is no equivalent to the indefinite article, and *ān* 'one' is a numeral.

Perhaps the most unexpected feature of noun phrases is the position of preposition associated with the noun phrase. Although prepositions usually precede their associated noun phrase, they are quite often found in a position detached from that noun phrase. This phenomenon, usually called (preposition) **stranding**, is familiar enough in present-day English; compare (29) and (30), where the latter, with stranding, is more usual in informal speech:

(29) The house in which I live
(30) The house I live in

Stranding is particularly frequent in relative clauses in Old English, as in (31), cf. (23):

(31) sumne dæl þæs mēoses þe hēo mid beweaxen wæs
some part of the moss which it with covered was

Note, however, that the stranded preposition does not disturb the position of the verb.

However, and this is quite clearly different from present-day English, there is a range of other contexts in which stranding occurs. Here is another example with verb-final structure:

(32) ond þā gatu him tō belocen hæfdon
and the gates them to locked were [... were locked against them]

Yet the preposition can also, indeed frequently, be stranded in simple sentences where stranding would be impossible today:

(33) hē cwæð him tō
he spoke him to

Such stranding occurs only with pronouns and it is particularly frequent when the preposition is *tō*, although other prepositions can do the same, especially if they are disyllabic. The source of the structure is not known, but it is probably associated with weight. Note that there is a relic of the construction in present-day English in a form such as *therein*; compare the parallel Old English form *þǣrinne*.

I shall not explore other differences in any of the above areas, for although there are many, they are mostly of only minor significance and they can usually be easily understood.

7.5 Negation

One of the most distinctive features of Old English in comparison with not only present-day English but also other Germanic languages together with other western languages such as French and Spanish on the one hand and Welsh and Gaelic on the other is its methods of negation. True enough, the simple negative particle *ne* behaves exactly as might be expected. That is to say, when a verb is negated the negative particle precedes the verb. The negative often behaves as the first element in the clause, and therefore the following is a typical example:

(34) Ne cōm hē
not came he

It should be apparent from (34) that not only does *ne* precede the verb, but also that there is no sign of any dummy auxiliary verb as would be found today, as in *he did not come*.

The most remarkable feature of negation in Old English, however, is that seen in a sentence such as:

(35) *Ne* mētte hē ǣr *nān* ġebūn land
not found he earlier *no* occupied land

This, of course, looks like the non-standard forms of present-day English which are quite widely found everywhere in Britain, as in *he didn't buy nothing*, i.e. 'he didn't buy anything'. The similarity is not accidental. The standard forms of today show one of the few successful attempts at prescriptivism. On the other hand the non-standard forms demonstrate a direct line of descent from Old English.

The general, but not absolute, usage in Old English was that in negative clauses *ne* appeared before the finite verb and that it also attached itself to any suitable indefinite pronoun or quantifier. The usual name for this construction is **negative concord**, rather than multiple negation, for the latter could imply that each negative element had its own effect (the false claim of the prescriptivists). But negative concord shows that the actual effect is that negation spreads from an initial negation to any other items which can take the particle.

Negative concord is by no means restricted to one further instance of the particle. As an example of extended concord, consider the following example:

(36) ... ðā ðā wē hit *nōh*wæðer *ne* selfe *ne* lufedon, *ne* ēac ōðrum monnum *ne* lēfdon
... when we it neither not selves not loved, nor also to other men not allowed
'when we neither loved it ourselves, nor even allowed it to others'

Very often the negative particle is cliticised, or attached to the following word. This process can be seen in the *nān* of (35) and the *nōhwæðer* of (36). The cliticisation to indefinite pronouns is probably clear enough. But there is also cliticisation to the following verb under certain conditions. The verbs affected are *wesan* 'be', *wile* 'will', *witan* 'know', *habban* 'have', *āgan* 'own/owe'. These verbs share the property of starting with either /w/, /h/ or a vowel, but interestingly they are all, with the exception of *witan*, which has been lost, related to present-day auxiliary verbs. This is even true of *āgan*, which develops into *ought*. No other verbs show the cliticisation, not even *weorþan* 'become', and forms of *bēon* (as opposed to *wesan*) do not cliticise either, since they begin with the consonant /b/. This cliticisation is normally called negative contraction, and typical examples of it are seen in:

(37) Ac hē *nyste* hwæt þæs sōþes wæs
But he didn't know how true that was
(38) *Næfde* hē þēah mā ðonne twentiġ hryðera
He didn't have, however, more than twenty cows
(39) Ac heora tal *næs* nā of rihtwīsnysse ac of nīðe
But their story wasn't at all of truth but of evil

7.6 Relative and other clauses

After the interruption of §7.5, due to the necessity of discussing a topic which is so salient in Old English that I couldn't delay its introduction any longer, let me now return to clause structure. The first issue that has to be considered here concerns three methods by which clauses may be linked together, namely **coordination, parataxis** and **hypotaxis**. Each of these is important in Old English.

The easiest of these, because it is the most familiar, is undoubtedly coordination, in which two main, or independent, clauses are linked together by a coordinating conjunction. The most obvious examples use the conjunction *and* 'and', but Old English deployed a wide range of conjunctions. The following example is both typical and interesting:

(40) Ond se Cynewulf oft miclum ġefeohtum feaht uuiþ [= wiþ]
      Bretwālum
      And this Cynewulf often great fights fought against the Welsh

The example is interesting because there is verb-final word order (the final phrase being where it is because of considerations of weight). It is a feature of such clauses that verb-final order is common. You may also have noticed that in this example there is actually no coordination, but instead merely a simple clause.

Parataxis is a kind of halfway house between coordination and hypotaxis, where the latter involves overt subordination. In parataxis there is a relationship between a main clause and a subordinate clause, but crucially there is no overt signal of subordination, except that there is no overt subject. Thus the second clause in the following example lacks an overt subject, which would be identical with the subject of the first clause:

(41) þā cōmon þēofas eahta, woldon stelan þā māðmas
      Then came eight thieves, wanted to steal the treasures

Very often the verbs in such structures correspond to present participles in present-day English:

(42) Hē sæt on ðǣm muntum, wēop ond hearpode
      He sat on the mountain tops, weeping and playing the harp

Hypotaxis, or subordination, is used extensively in Old English, often together with **correlation**, where two (or more) clauses are linked together by means of correlative elements. Thus we find examples such as the following, where the subordinate clause is first introduced by *þā* 'when' and the main clause by *þā* 'then'. Note that which clause is which is most easily determined by verb-final order against verb-second order:

(43) þā hē ðā þās andsware onfēng, þā ongon hē sōna singan
      When he then that answer received, then began he at once to
      sing

It is tempting to spend much more time on correlative structures, of which the Old English writers were clearly fond, at least in the rather literary texts which dominate the available material. But time presses. Instead let me focus attention on relative clauses, which show clear differences from relative clauses today. In particular I want to look at methods used to introduce the relative clause, namely various types of what are nowadays grouped together as **complementisers**.

Essentially there were two relative complementisers possible in Old English, together with some examples where there is no complementiser at all. As I shall show, it is also possible to find compound-type structures with both complementisers used, in a strictly-defined sequence. Perhaps most surprising of all is the fact that Old English had neither the *who*-nor the *that*-pronoun of the present-day language, although in relation to that, this suggestion only messily relates to the Old English situation, as I discuss immediately below.

Instead, the two relative complementisers in Old English are firstly what we may call the **relative particle** *þe*, which is indeclinable, and secondly the demonstrative pronoun *se, þæt, sēo* used as a relative pronoun. A straightforward example of the particle is:

(44) Þā becōm hē tō Westseaxan, *þe* wæs ðā ġyt hæþen
      Then he went to Wessex, which was then still heathen

whilst here is an example with two relative clauses in consecutive clauses, each having a different form of the relative pronoun:

(45) Se hearpere wæs unġefræġlīċe good, ðæs nama wæs Orfeus
      The harper was incredibly good, whose name was Orpheus
(46) Hē hæfde ān swīðe ænliċ wīf, sīo wæs hāten Eurudiċe
      He had a very excellent wife, who was called Eurydice

The use of the demonstrative pronoun as a relative, although now perhaps alien to English, unless one assumes that the demonstrative pronoun is directly, rather than indirectly, developed as a relative, will be recognisable to anyone who has some knowledge of present-day German.

In many instances the use of demonstrative alone could be confusing, since there is the possibility that it might be a simple demonstrative rather than a relative; on the other hand the use of the relative particle alone can be unhelpful, since it is uninflected. These difficulties are resolved by a sequence of pronoun + particle, as in:

(47) Þriwa ċlypode sēo [FEM] stemn from þære ðrynesse sēo [FEM] þe
      is ælmihtiġ god

Three times called the voice from the Trinity which is almighty
God

Sometimes, however, there is a further difficulty, for the pronoun can, by
a process called relative attraction, take the case not of the relative but
rather that of its antecedent:

(48) Heriað forðī Drihten [ACC], þone [ACC] ðe eardað on Sīon
      Praise therefore the Lord, who that lives in Zion

And occasionally we find examples where there is no relative element
present at all:

(49) And on þys ilcan ḡēre forðferde Æþered wæs on Defenum
      ealdorman
      And in this same year died Athered, (who) was Alderman of
      Devon

Such structures are often described as contact clauses, since they have no
complementiser intervening between the two clauses.

7.7 Impersonal verbs

There is much more that could be said about clause structure, both in
detail and in variety, but, as always, a line must be drawn somewhere,
and this seems an appropriate place to draw it. A simple reason for this
is that there is one further feature of Old English syntax which must be
discussed before we move on to matters of vocabulary in Chapter 8. This
is the matter of impersonal verbs.

Consider the following present-day English sentence:

(50) It is raining

Such an example is often described as having an impersonal verb structure. What we mean by that is that the subject, *it*, is not a full subject, for
it has no meaning; its only purpose is to fill the otherwise empty subject
position, which every finite clause requires to be filled. *It*, therefore, is a
dummy subject inserted to fulfil the demands of present-day syntax.

Compare with (50) the following Old English sentence:

(51) Norþan snīwde
      From the north snowed

Here we can see that it isn't obligatory for an Old English sentence to
have a subject. If you know Latin, then such 'omission' of the subject may
be familiar to you.

There would be no need to make any fuss about such impersonal verbs if the only verbs which were involved were the so-called weather verbs like *snow* and *rain* and if there were no further consequences. Then the same situation would exist in Old English as in present-day English. But that is not the case.

Rather, in Old English there is a range of verbs which can occur without a subject in the nominative case, although there is often the possibility of these verbs also occurring with a 'normal' subject. I shall ignore that variation for a moment, but you should remember that it is possible and even, in later texts, more and more frequent. The verbs which participate in impersonal constructions, apart from the weather verbs, tend to share semantic features relating to physical or mental experiences. This can be seen in an example such as the following:

(52) him [DAT] ofhrēow þæs mannes [GEN]
      he experienced pity because of the man [to him was pity because of the man]

The best way to explain what happens is by taking two semantic concepts, namely **experiencer** and **cause**, where the experiencer is an animate noun and the cause either a noun phrase or a clause. In (51) there neither an experiencer nor a cause, just as in the present-day example (50). This type is usually called a zero-place impersonal. On the other hand, in (52) *him* is the experiencer and *þæs mannes* the cause; this is a two-place impersonal. It is also possible to obtain one-place impersonals:

(53) Longað hine [ACC] hearde
      he longs grievously

The general rule for all impersonal constructions is that the experiencer is in either the accusative or the dative case, whilst the cause, if a noun phrase, is in the genitive case.

Clearly, as noun morphology began, if not to disappear, at least to lose some of its crucial case distinctions, then examples such as (51) would begin, also, to look strange, for the norm would be for something which had both the morphological properties of a subject and the positional place of a subject to have the normal case of a subject, namely the nominative. Thus alongside (51) we find both the following types:

(54) þā ofhrēow ðām munece [DAT] þæs hreoflian mǣgenlēast [NOM]
      Then pitied the monk the leper's feebleness
(55) Se mæsseprēost [NOM] þæs mannes [GEN] ofhrēow
      The priest for the man felt pity

These variations, however, demonstrate that the use of impersonal constructions can highlight semantic differences which have to be handled by very different constructions in present-day English. In both (54) and (55) we would be most likely to use the phrasal construction *feel pity*, as in:

(56) The leper's feebleness caused the monk to feel pity (for him)
(57) The priest felt pity for the man

I am conscious that the above account scarcely scratches the surface of the subject, but perhaps there is sufficient here for you to see that impersonals are not only quite unlike any structure in present-day English, but that there is much work to be done to explain the developments which eventually bring us to the situation today. And as a final aside it may be noted that there are still a very few idiomatic and plainly archaic forms around, notably *methinks* for *I think*.

Exercise

So far I have presented texts from both the time of Alfred and the time of Ælfric and Wulfstan. In this exercise I have taken an extract from just before the Norman Conquest. There are two reasons for this choice: one historical, one linguistic. Historically I have chosen an extract from the *Anglo-Saxon Chronicles* which outlines some of the internal fighting that occurred during the reign of Edward the Confessor, and therefore serves as a brief insight into the kinds of issue which were to lead to the disappearance of the Anglo-Saxon kingdom.

Linguistically, although undoubtedly little has been lost from the classical forms of Old English, there are a few signs in this extract of the changes which begin to occur after the Norman Conquest. You should, therefore, pay special attention to forms which show developments which reflect the way in which the language is already beginning to change. In addition, since in this chapter we have mostly been concerned with word order, you should examine each clause and the word order used there. This passage is written in a relatively non-literary style and consists of quite short clauses, so there is a considerable amount of material to examine.

And cōm þā Eustatius fram ġeondan sǣ sōna æfter þām bisċop and ġewende tō ðām cynge, and spæc wið hine þæt þæt hē þā wolde and ġewende þā hāmweard.

Ðā hē cōm tō Cantwarbyriġ ēast, þā snædde hē þǣr, and his menn, and tō Dofran ġewende. þā hē wæs sume mīla oððe māre beheonan Dofran, þā dyde hē on his byrnan and his ġefēran ealle, and fōran tō Dofran.

þā hī þider cōmon, þā woldon hī innian hī þǣr heom sylfan ġelīcode. þā cōm ān his manna and wolde wīcian æt ānes bundan hūse his unðances, and ġewundode þone hūsbūndon, and se hūsbūnda ofslōh þone ōðerne. Ðā wearð Eustatius uppon his horse, and his ġefēran upon heora, and fērdon tō þām hūsbūndon and ofslōgon hine binnan his āġenan heorðe, and wendon him þā up tō þǣre burġe weard, and ofslōgon ǣġðer ġe wiðinnan ġewiðūtan mā þanne xx manna. And þā burhmenn ofslōgon xix menn on ōðre healfe and ġewundoden þæt hī nystan hū fela.

8 Vocabulary

8.1 The sources of vocabulary

If we examine almost any random sample of present-day English, what we shall find is a mixture of linguistic sources. The following, for example, is from the beginning of Graham Greene's *Stamboul Train* (Heinemann, 1932):

> The *purser* **took** the last landing-*card* in his hand and watched the *passengers cross* the grey wet *quay*, over a wilderness of *points* and *rails*, *round* the *corners* of *abandoned* <u>trucks</u>.

The italicised words are of French origin, whilst *took* is from Scandinavian and *trucks* from Latin. Perhaps about thirty per cent of present-day vocabulary is of French origin, and there are significantly large proportions of our vocabulary from other languages. In particular, there are exceptionally important words of Scandinavian origin, even although they are not nearly as numerous as the French words. Thus core grammatical items such as *they*, *are* and *she* are all Scandinavian as are the body-part nouns *leg* and *neck* and the kinship term *sister*.

The picture presented above, which ignores many of the words in the present-day language whose origin lies in other languages, for example Dutch *sketch*, but often from even more distant languages, such as *shampoo* from Hindi or *wigwam* from the North American language Ojibwa, is in stark contrast to the situation in Old English. For there the overwhelming majority of words are of native, Germanic, origin; none of the words I have mentioned above formed part of Old English vocabulary, not even the Scandinavian grammatical items. Those terms replaced the Old English words *hī*, *synd* and *hēo* during the Middle English period.

As I shall show later, there are words of non-native origin in Old English, the vast majority of which are from Latin. It has been estimated only about 3 per cent of Old English vocabulary is taken from non-native sources and it is clear that the strong preference in Old English was to use its native resources in order to create new vocabulary. In this respect, therefore, and as elsewhere, Old English is typically Germanic.

We can classify Old English vocabulary into the following four types. Firstly, native core vocabulary; secondly, **affixation**, the process by which a native affix is attached to an existing word to create a new word, as in present-day English *brightness* from *bright* plus the suffix *-ness*; thirdly, **compounding**, the process by which two independent words are joined together to create a new third word, as in present-day *railway*, created from the two dependent words *rail* and *way*; fourthly, **borrowing**, that is to say introducing non-native words into the language in exactly the way we have already seen. Such words are often called **loan words**, although neither the term 'borrowing' nor the term 'loan word' has exactly the correct meaning. The second and third types, i.e. affixation and compounding, can be taken together as **word-formation**.

8.2 Core vocabulary

It might be thought entirely reasonable to assume that there is nothing to be said about core vocabulary other than the simple fact that this set consists virtually entirely of items shared with all or some of the other Germanic languages. However, it is appropriate to consider in this context a number of types of word formation which are essentially historical in nature and which were already in Old English, to a greater or lesser extent, no longer productive processes.

What I mean by this is that there appears to have been a wealth of word-formation processes in earlier Germanic and even more so in Indo-European. In the course of time most of these fell into disuse. However the words so formed naturally remained in the language and therefore the process remains recognisable. It can be quite difficult to decide whether or not some particular word-formation process remains synchronically active, especially when we are dealing with an ancient language such as Old English where, what is more, the textual evidence is patchy. Therefore some of the cases I discuss below might easily be taken under the heading of affixation.

Perhaps the most obvious of these older formations concerns Ablaut. So far my discussion of Ablaut has been restricted to verb types, but originally Ablaut was a more widespread phenomenon by which nouns could be formed from strong verbs, so that we find *bite* 'a bite' formed from the verb *bītan*, using the ablaut variant normally associated with the past plural of verbs. Other examples are based on the present tense, for example *wito* 'wise man' from *witan* 'know'.

There are more complex examples than these, for in many cases the word-formation interacts with historical sound changes. The most important concern Verner's Law, which I discussed in Chapter 5 and *i*-mutation (see the discussion in §4.5). But these changes can obscure the relation between the original verb and its derived noun. A typical example of the former is *cyre* 'choice' from *ċēosan* 'choose', and *cyme* 'arrival' from *cuman* 'come' is typical of the latter. It is even possible to find examples where both changes have occurred, as in *hryre* 'fall' from *hrēosan* 'fall'. It is also possible to find more than one noun derived from a single verb. Thus alongside *cyme* 'arrival' we also find *cuma* 'guest'.

Strong verbs are not the only verbs from which nouns can be derived. Weak verbs too can be used to form new nouns. This happens both with weak class 1 verbs, so that we find *dōm* 'judgement' from *dēman* 'judge', and class 2 verbs, so that we find *lufu* 'love' from *lufian* 'love'.

As I said earlier, this derivation type largely belongs to an early stage in Germanic, and begins to be lost as the relationship between verb and noun becomes obscured. This is least true of weak class 2 verbs, where few historical changes intervene in the way that Verner's Law and *i*-mutation do. This remains, therefore, an active word-formation process in Old English. It may, indeed, be the source of the Ø-formative or **conversion** process of present-day English, whereby a word is formed without any overt affixation, for example $desire_v \rightarrow desire_N$, compare $love_v \sim love_N$ and the Old English forms above.

It is not only nouns that can be formed by the above processes, for adjectives too can be derived. Thus we find examples such as *full* 'full' from class 1 *fyllan* and *gōd* 'good' from class 2 *gōdian* 'make better'. Note that the class 1 examples show *i*-umlaut of the verb but not of the derived adjective. This is the same phenomenon that occurs with the derivation of nouns from class 1. Amongst other things this is good evidence that the derivational process was very early, certainly before the time of *i*-mutation.

The above account rather implies that there was not, in the earliest stages of Old English, any derivation of new verbs from nouns or adjectives. This is indeed largely, but not wholly, true. The only cases of new verbs which have a certain derivational status are associated with class 2 weak verbs, where, for example, we find *lufian* 'love' from the older noun *lufu* 'love'. In Old English itself this becomes a very frequent type of derivation, so that from *wuldor* 'glory' we find *wuldrian* 'glorify'. This can extend quite easily to words borrowed from Latin, so that we find new verbs such as *plantian* 'plant' from the borrowed noun.

8.3 Affixation

Affixation is by far the most frequent method for creating new vocabulary in Old English. There is a very large number of both **prefixes** and **suffixes** in the language, many of which are themselves very often used. Within the limits of this book it is rather difficult to give a good impression of the variety of affixation in use without descending into mere lists. I shall, therefore, restrict my comments to the most frequent of all the affixes, and to the principal features which mark out prefixes and suffixes.

When considering prefixes there is one phonological issue which needs to be addressed immediately. There is good evidence to suggest that in early Germanic only nouns could be inseparably prefixed, whilst with verbs the prefix could be separated from the verb. Then what happened is that the stress came to be fixed on the first syllable which could be the prefixed element. Whilst this was happening, the separable verbal prefixes remained separable, and therefore did not receive the fixed stress. Only at a later stage did the separable verbal prefixes become inseparable, but then it was too late for the fixed stress to be moved.

The consequence of this variation is that we find sets of forms such as: *sácan*$_V$ 'fight' ~ *ándsàca*$_N$ 'enemy' ~ *onsácan*$_V$ 'deny'. This variation may have contributed to the contrast in present-day English between, for example, *récòrd*$_N$ and *recórd*$_V$. It may also be helpful to consider the distinctions in both Dutch and German between **inseparable** and **separable** verbs. In both languages there is a major distinction between two types of prefixed verbs. Firstly there are verbs where the prefix always remains with the verbs, so that we find, for example, *Ich habe die Antwort vergessen* 'I have the answer forgotten'. But secondly there are verbs where the prefix is separated in the same type of construction. In that type we find *ge-* inserted between the prefix and the verb. Thus we find *Er ist zurückgekommen* 'He has back come'. In some instances in Old English the difference in stress is made apparent by the shape of the prefix, as can be seen in the examples of *ándsàca* and *onsácan* above.

Amongst prefixes, the most common one, indeed the most common of all affixes, is *ge-*. This prefix, especially, but by no means only, when prefixed to a past participle often seems to be empty of all semantic meaning, and can become close to being an inflectional marker rather than a prefix. When used as a true verbal prefix, its meaning is most often close to perfectivity, result or completion, as in *geascian* 'learn by asking'. It can also be used as a nominal prefix, as in *gefera* 'companion'. The most common meanings associated with the nominal prefix are collectivity, as in *ġescy* 'a pair of shoes', and associativity, as in *ġefera*. It should be noted that this prefix is never stressed, even in nominal contexts.

It is not always possible to give a clear indication of meaning to some of the prefixes. Thus *a-*, a verbal prefix found in verbs such as *acalan* 'become frozen', is clearly an intensifier of *calan* 'become cold', but *afysan* and *fysan* can both mean 'drive away'. Another similar case is *be-*, as in *bebēodan* 'offer', but again there are other examples with perfective or intensifying effect, such as *belucan* 'lock up'. Other prefixes can have more than one distinct meaning. An excellent example of this is *in-*. One meaning is quite transparent from a present-day perspective, since it is the same as that for 'in' today, hence *ingān* 'go in' and *inneweard* 'inward'. But it also has an intensifying meaning, as in *infrōd* 'very wise'.

One point which becomes quickly apparent is that very many of the Old English prefixes have been lost from the language since that time. Sometimes the loss is total, as in the case of *ġe-*; sometimes a few examples may remain, but often their prefixal status is not obvious, as in, for example *arise* from OE *arīsan*. Other cases still are misleading; for example the OE prefix *in-* should not be confused with the Latinate prefix *in-* as in *incomplete*. In later English there was considerable borrowing of prefixes from the Romance languages.

There was in Old English even more suffixation than prefixation. One general issue is whether a given suffix remained synchronically active in Old English or was rather a relic of a system which was active only in the Germanic period or even earlier. Thus it is far from clear that a derived form such as *lengð* 'length' (from *leng* + *ð*) represents a relic or a still active derivational process; the same is perhaps true of present-day *length*, although there are further complications with that form which are outside the present work.

Some of the Old English suffixes remain in frequent use today. Thus we find *grǣdiġ* 'greed' with the suffix *-iġ*. This suffix is in competition with the suffix *-liċ* found in, for example, *dēopliċ* 'deeply'. So both *cræftiġ* and *cræftlic* 'strong' therefore occur. In addition, alternative suffixes may have become prevalent later, hence *ċildlic* and *cildisc* 'childish' both occur, but the latter wins out (but note *child-like*).

There are also other distinguishing features amongst suffixes. Grammatically, as with prefixes, we can isolate nominal suffixes, such as *-scipe*, which forms nouns from nouns, for example *frēondscipe* 'friendship', adjectival suffixes such as in *grǣdiġ* above, and others which change the part of speech, as in *hæbbend* 'owner' from *habban* 'have'. Morphological classification accounts for the variation between *bodung* 'preaching' from class 2 *bodian* and *ċyping* 'trade' from class 1 *ċypan* 'sell'. There are also sometimes differences between dialects. For example female agentive nouns in West Saxon regularly use the suffix *-estre* (equivalent to *-ess* in present-day English), and hence we find *huntiġestre* 'huntress', but in more northern dialects the usual form is with *-iċġe*, giving *huntiċġe*, both from *huntian* 'hunt'.

8.4 Compounds

In §8.3 I have given an outline of how prevalent and how varied is the extent of affixation in Old English. In comparing Old English and present-day English there is not much difference in the amount of affixation used, but only in the actual affixes involved. By quite early in the Middle English period many of the original Germanic affixes were lost – this is particularly true of prefixes where replacement by the verb + particle found in Scandinavian became dominant – but they were quickly replaced by new affixes from Latin and French.

On the other hand, an even more striking feature about Old English vocabulary is the number of compounds used, for, as I shall show, the number of compounds used in Old English far exceeds the number used in any later period (notwithstanding the fact that the last century or so has seen a considerable rise in the use of compounds).

As we shall see in the next chapter, the distribution of compounds in Old English is rather skewed. It is certainly true that every genre of Old English demonstrates compounding, and hence it is true that it is a native and productive process. Nevertheless, compounding is particularly frequent in poetry, where there is a large demand for alternative synonyms or near synonyms, for reasons I shall discuss later. In the 3,182 lines of *Beowulf*, for example, there are 903 distinct compounds, that is to say, there is a new compound in, approximately, every third line of the poem.

What makes something a **compound**? If we examine a present-day word such as *railway*, how can we tell that this is a compound rather than either a simple word or word plus an affix? The answer to that lies in the fact that this word itself contains two independent words, namely *rail* and *way*. That is to say, a compound is formed from existing words, two, or even more, as in *railway station*. Note that this last example shows that spelling, including, although not here, hyphenation, is not a reliable guide. The same holds for Old English.

A second issue of definition is important, namely what is the relation between the two words which are compounded? If we look at *railway* it clearly refers to a kind of *way*, and similarly *railway station* refers to a kind of *station*. This points to the view that the second element is the **head** of the compound which the first element modifies. You may have thought of examples which apparently contradict this, for example a *paperback* is not a kind of *back*, but a book with paper covers. Such examples, where neither the head of the compound nor the modifier is the referent of the compound, are called **bahuvrihi** compounds, a term originating with the Sanskrit grammarians of ancient India. Bahuvrihi compounds are at least as common in Old English as today.

Let us now move on to Old English compounds themselves. The most common examples involve noun+noun compounds, such as *bōccræft* 'book-craft' = 'literature' and *wīfmann* 'woman'. The latter example serves to show why the compound is masculine in gender, because it is the head noun, here *mann*, which determines the gender of the compound noun. Sometimes the first noun is in the genitive case, as in *Englalond* 'England, land of the Angles', and it could be argued, but with less probability, that these are not genuine compounds but simply syntactic groups.

Noun compounds are also formed with both adjectival and with adverbial modifiers. Typical examples of the former include *hāliġdæġ* 'holy day' (cf. *holiday*) and *wildgōs* 'wild goose'; for the latter there are many examples parallel in structure to *forþfæder* 'forefather' and *oferbrǣw* 'eyebrow'. Occasionally we find noun compounds consisting of three words (compare *railway station* above), as in *niht-butorflēoġe* 'night butter-fly' = 'moth'.

Turning now to adjective compounds, here too the modifier may be either a noun, an adjective or an adverb. Since these types are, for the most part, not different in principle from the noun compounds I have just discussed, I need only cite a few examples. Thus we find *dōmġeorn* 'eager for glory', *ealmihtiġ* 'almighty' and *eftboren* 'born again'. Nevertheless there are some less-expected formations. One such type consists of a manner adverb plus an adjective, as in *dēoppancol* 'deeply thinking' = 'contemplative', a type which does not occur today. Another interesting group has a present participle as the head, for example *ealodrincende* 'beer-drinking', a formation which is very active in the present day as well.

One recurrent problem in the treatment of Old English compounding and affixation is that it is not always easy to determine whether a particular item is part of a compound or rather an affix. For example, consider the word *wīsdom* 'wisdom'. At first sight it looks certain that *-dom* is a suffix, for there are many other examples such as *lǣċedom* 'medicine' and *pēowdom* 'slavery'. But there is a problem, for there exists also the simple independent word *dōm* and this can also occur as the first part of a compound, as in *dōmġeorn* 'glory-eager' or *dōmdæġ* 'doom-day'. The line between compounding and affixation, therefore, may be rather fuzzy. An element such as *-dom* is often referred to as a **suffixoid** because of its rather intermediate status. Other possible suffixoids include *-had* 'hood', *-lac* with a rather general meaning of 'act' or 'state', as in *rēaflac* 'robbery', that is 'act of robbing', similarly *-rǽden* in *camprǽden* 'fighting' from *campian* 'fight'. There are adjectival suffixoids too, for example *-fǽst* and *-least*.

Compounds where the head is a verb show a striking contrast with present-day English, although not, it should be pointed out, with either Dutch or German. For here a concept I have already mentioned, namely that of separable and inseparable verbs, comes into play. In compound verbs the modifying element is either an adverb or a preposition. Thus we find examples such as *æfterfolgian* 'pursue'. That seems simple enough, but I should emphasise the importance of understanding the difference between these two types of verb, as outlined above.

But compare *oferfeohtan* 'conquer' and *forþbrengan* 'bring forth' when, for instance, they occur with *tō* 'in order to': what we find is *tō oferfeohtanne* but *forþ tō brenganne*. If, as is the case with *forþbrengan*, there is a particle, including not only a particle such as *tō* but also the negator *ne*, then the particle intervenes between the two parts of the compound. The first element may also be placed after the verb. It is possible to group such constructions into separable and inseparable categories, but there is also a large group which falls into both categories, often, but not always, with a difference in meaning. By the very end of the Old English period there are signs that verbal constructions are about to be lost, only few types remaining, with the rise of the modern verb-particle construction. The variation in Old English between inseparable *understándan* 'understand' and separable *únderstàndan* 'stand under' is at most only opaquely preserved today.

8.5 Latin loans

As I mentioned at the beginning of this chapter, there was in Old English only a very limited use of words taken from other languages, i.e. borrowed or loan words, and those words were primarily from Latin. Apart from Latin, Old English borrowed words from the Scandinavian languages after the Viking invasions, from the Celtic languages mostly at a very early date, and there was also a scattering of forms from the other Germanic languages. At the very end of the period we begin to see the first loan words from Norman French.

The obvious place to start, therefore, is with Latin. Writers often talk about Latin loans being in three groups: (1) continental period; (2) settlement period; (3) Christian period. In fact it is probably preferable to divide the last of these into two further periods, but I shall discuss that later. Firstly, however, let us examine the first group. This consists of words borrowed into one or more different Germanic dialects, including the predecessors of Old English, from about the time of Julius Caesar onwards. Clearly they are the result of contact between the Germanic tribes and the expanding and dominating Roman Empire. These loan words come from diverse areas of vocabulary (although in terms of grammar nouns greatly predominate, but this is the case with all loans during the Old English period), which is a good indication of the widespread influence of the Empire. A representative listing of words would include, perhaps, *candel*, 'candle', *catte* 'cat', *elpend* 'elephant', *planta* 'plant', *strǣt* 'road' and, a verbal example, *ċȳpan* 'buy'. Many such examples come not from classical Latin, but from Vulgar Latin, the form of the language likely to have been used by the ordinary soldiers and camp-followers.

It is estimated that Old English contained about 170 Latin loans due to pre-settlement, that is continental, borrowing. During the first two or three centuries following the settlement of Britain, rather fewer Latin loans were borrowed. If the withdrawal of the Roman Empire in 410 was accompanied by the immediate loss of Latin as the official language, then the number of new loans accepted by the new Germanic invaders would have been minimal. But even if Latin remained, as is perhaps more likely, at least for a time, it would, in Britain, have been associated in the minds of the new invaders with a subordinate group, namely the Celtic aristocracy and a few Latin speakers left behind in towns. The extent to which the settlement period should be distinguished from the continental period remains an open question. A few words certainly stem from this time, of which the best known is undoubtedly *ċeaster* 'castle', because of its frequent use in place-names.

I mentioned above that loans from the period of Christianity can usefully be divided into two groups. The first group belongs to the first two or three centuries after the wholesale adoption of Christianity in the seventh century. The Latin loans borrowed in this period are mostly of a political nature, that is to say they tend to be forms associated with the organisation of the church, rather than with the concepts of the new faith itself. Thus we find words such as *abbod* 'abbot', *mæsse* 'mass', *offrian* 'offer'. An extension of this consists of words related to learning, for example *scōl* 'school', together with a few words of a more general nature, hence *caul* 'cabbage'. On the other hand *hǣlend* 'Saviour', an entirely native word, was used for Christ, rather than Latin *dominus*.

The second group of post-settlement Latin loans are, above all, associated with the period of the Benedictine monastic revival which occurred in the second half of the tenth century. These loans are normally quite different in character from any of the earlier loans, often reflecting a different register of language, that is to say, they reflect a form of language most suited to formal and highly educated language, rather than the language of everyday speech, where the earlier loans usually sat comfortably.

This difference is apparent in both the original language and Old English. As far as Latin is concerned, these new loans regularly come not from Vulgar Latin, as previously, but rather from the writers of Classical Latin. This is demonstrated by the linguistic forms themselves and it further implies that these new loans are part of the written rather than the spoken language, a clear contrast with the earlier situation. In terms of Old English we find that these new loans are not always well assimilated into the language, so that they retain most or all of their Latin structure. Furthermore, it is sometimes the case that a new word in fact replicates an earlier loan of the same original word, but showing a Classical, rather than a Vulgar, Latin form and without most of the changes which occurred in the transition to Old English. A quite typical example of this process is *tabele* 'table' alongside earlier *tæfl*.

Although many of these new loans are religious in nature, for example *apostata* 'apostate' and *sabbat* 'Sabbath', others reflect the general world of learning, and in particular curiosity about foreign lands. This latter accounts for words such as *cucumer* 'cucumber' and *delfin* 'dolphin'. The formal nature of the new vocabulary can be seen in examples where the Latin word replaces an Old English one, as in *grammaticcræft* 'grammar' for native *stæfcræft*.

Borrowings from Latin can take other forms than those discussed above. One particular type is that of semantic loans. The basic shape of such a loan is where the meaning of a Latin word is transferred to an English word which did not originally have that meaning. For example, the word *tunge* 'tongue' had at first only the meaning of the body part, but under the influence of Latin *lingua*, which has not only that meaning but also the meaning 'language', it also acquired the meaning 'language'. A slightly different type is found in Latin *discipulus* 'disciple', for in that case what happened was that the Latin meaning was transferred to English *cniht* 'boy, servant'. In late Old English we also find what are called loan translations, where a new complex expression is created in imitation of a Latin complex expression. Thus we find, for example, Latin *praepositio* 'proposition' turned into English *forsetnys*.

8.6 Other loan words

There are only a few hundred Latin loan words in Old English, and as I have shown, a great many of these, perhaps a third, are restricted to formal registers, which includes not only technical writing but also Latin–Old English glossaries. Nevertheless these loans provide the bulk of loan words in Old English. The only other substantial group of loans are, as I have said, from Scandinavian. Let us now therefore turn to these.

It is well-known that eventually English acquired a great many important words, including even function words such as *are*, from the Scandinavian languages. But it is also well-known that the overwhelming majority of these words only begin to be found after the end of the Old English period. Any discussion of Scandinavian loans is complicated by the fact that two closely-related languages are involved. On the one hand there is Danish, whose speakers occupied the north-east, Yorkshire and down to East Anglia; on the other there is Norwegian, found in the north-west.

Perhaps the first substantial evidence of Scandinavian influence is to be found with place-names, although we mostly have to rely here on the evidence of the *Domesday Book*, composed after the Norman Conquest. Thus we find Danish suffixes such as *-by* 'village' or *-þorp* 'farm' and Norwegian *-þweit* 'clearing' which eventually appear in place-names such as *Derby*, *Scunthorpe* and *Satterthwaite*. The place-name evidence is important as proof of the degree of contact between the English and the Scandinavians, but it does not necessarily prove the assimilation of large numbers of loan words into the ordinary language.

Many of the early Scandinavian loans are, naturally, associated with seafaring, so we find *hæfene* 'haven', *lending* 'a landing', *stēoresman* 'pilot'. Others are legal terms, as a result of the Danelaw settlement, including the word *lagu* 'law' itself, and connected with that is *feolagu* 'fellow'. Many of these words are to become common, for example *hūsbonda* 'house-holder', but others have either been lost or become restricted in use, e.g. *carl* 'man'. There are a few verbs which have been borrowed, for example *eggian* 'egg on', *hittan* 'hit'.

Turning to other sources, perhaps the most striking feature is how few words appear to have been borrowed from Celtic. It is true that many place-names, of rivers, for example, retain their Celtic name; in the case of *Avon* that name is widespread throughout Britain. There is a socio-linguistic explanation for this, namely that the Celtic peoples formed a subordinate group within the new Anglo-Saxon society, and hence their language was shunned. Indeed, we can look at the position of Welsh today for confirmation that things need not change, even over centuries.

Settlement words borrowed from Celtic include *dunn* 'dun' and *broc* 'badger'. Irish missionaries were extremely influential in the spread of Christianity, and even if they regularly spoke Latin, they introduced a few words from their native tongue, of which the most frequent is *drȳ* 'magician'. Present-day *cross* is almost certainly a borrowing, possibly very late in the period, since in Old English it did not replace the native *rōd* 'rood'.

Almost all French loans into English either occur after the Conquest or during the preceding reign of Edward the Confessor. For the most part, therefore, they belong more obviously to the Middle English period. This is clearly true of words such as *cancelere* 'chancellor', *castel* 'castle' and *prisun* 'prison', which are all very late in terms of Old English. *Prȳt* 'pride' is a French loan which is often noted for its rather early use in Wulfstan's *Sermo Lupi ad Anglos*.

From the other Germanic languages we know of a handful of words which appear to have been borrowed from Old Saxon. These include *striδ* 'struggle' and *sūht* 'illness'. We know about these words because they appear in a poem called *Genesis B*, which is a translation from Old Saxon. But whether these are genuine loans, the result of close dialectal contact, or accidentally missing from other texts is hard to decide. The compound *īġland* 'island' may be a singular borrowing from Frisian.

Exercise

For this passage I have returned to Wulfstan's *Sermo Lupi ad Anglos*, not because of its inherent literary merits, which are considerable, but because this passage will exercise all your skills at deciphering all the types of word formation I have been discussing in this chapter, including loan words. By the end you will have a fair idea of how the Anglo-Saxons were able to use all these resources for rhetorical effect.

Nis ēac nān wundor þēah ūs mislimpe, for þām wē witan ful ġeorne þæt nū fela ġēara mænn nā ne rōhtan foroft hwæt hȳ worhtan wordes oδδe dǣde: ac werδ þes þēodsċipe, swā hit þinċan mæġ, swyδe forsyngod þurh mæniġfealde synna and þurh fela misdǣda; þurh morδdǣda and þurh mandǣda, þurh ġītsunga and þurh ġīfernessa, þurh stala and þurh strūdunga, þurh mannsylena and þurh hǣþene unsida, þurh swicdomas and þurh searacræftas, þurh lahbrycas and þurh ǣswicas, þurh mǣġrǣsas and þurh manslyhtas, þurh hādbrycas and ǣwbrycas, þurh sibleġeru and þurh mistliċe forliġru. And ēac syndan wīde, swā wē ǣr cwǣdan, þurh āδbricas and þurh wedbrycas and þurh mistliċe lēasunga forlōren and forloġen mā þonne sċolde;

and frēolsbricas and fæstenbrycas wīde ġeworhte oft and ġelōme. And ēac hēr syn on eared apostatan ābroþene and ċyriċhatan hetole and lēodhatan grimme ealles tō maneġe, and oferhogan wīde godcunra rihtlaga and crīstenra þēawa, and hōcorwyrde dysiġe ǣġhwǣr on þēode oftost on þā þing þe Godes bodan bēodaþ, and swyþost on þā þing þe ǣfre tō Godes lage ġebyriaþ mid rihte.

9 Variety

9.1 Introduction

The distance in time and the relatively small (compared with most later periods) amount of Old English text available to us can both lead us to the unfortunate view that Old English was a somewhat unvarying mass. This view can be further exaggerated by the texts by which any introductory work, such as this, defines itself. This definition finds expression in detail as much as in overall pattern. Thus, for example, in presenting inflectional patterns I have almost always restricted myself to a single pattern for any given set of forms. This may be inevitable, because an attempt to give even a small proportion of variant forms would tend to confuse rather than illuminate.

This chapter, therefore, is an attempt to demonstrate that there was significant variation in the Old English period. I shall try to prove the case by looking at four different areas: (1) chronology; (2) prose; (3) poetry; (4) dialect. Having said that, it is also impossible to ignore the presence of areas where there is no variation. Such lack of variation arises from more than one source, but overall the lack results from the fact that we are dealing with a language which exists only in written form. As a result, virtually every text is composed in a formal style. That is to say, we have no texts which are colloquial or deliberately reflect the spoken language, although in, for example, the text presented at the end of Chapter 7 I tried to remedy that in part. In §9.3 I shall mention a further example, but it should be seen as genuinely exceptional.

Other related missing variations include class features and gender features. The texts which we have are the product of an aristocratic or religious group, which reflects the state of literacy during the period. Even a reformer such as Alfred the Great was only interested in educating the elite of his society. This should not be read as a complaint but merely as a sign of the time. Thus we do not know whether the unlettered peasant used language in a form close to that of his 'betters'. The working class, to use an anachronistic term, was, literally, silent. Nor were the benefits of literacy extended to women, so they too remain as silent witnesses to the form of English at the time. So here, as elsewhere, we have to make do with what we have.

9.2 Chronology

English, as you now know, was first brought to Britain around the first part of the fifth century. However, apart from a few fragments, texts only begin to appear regularly around AD 700. These texts, however, are mostly very short. It is usual to suggest that the first flourishing of texts is just before and just after 900, under the encouragement of Alfred. In terms of West Saxon that is certainly true, although there are some important Mercian texts spread over the preceding two centuries. It becomes a little clearer, therefore, why the impression of an unvarying mass tends to prevail.

Even within West Saxon, however, there are signs of distinct differences beginning to appear within the relatively short time of the available texts. Inevitably, given the amount of material we have, these changes can appear as minor details, but I want simply to take two cases and show how these are clear indications of change in progress. Both these cases involve morphology, one relating to verbs, the other to nouns.

It will be recalled from Chapter 4 that there were two principal classes of weak verbs, class 1, as in *trymman* 'perform', and class 2, as in *lufian*. But within class 1 there was a sub-group of verbs like *nerian* 'save'. In an earlier chapter I mentioned that by the time of Ælfric verbs like this were beginning to adopt the forms of weak class 2, so that we find *nerað* rather than the expected *nereð*. In fact this process had already started, but in a very small way, at the time of Alfred.

So what we can see is a progression, the change becoming more widespread. And the change is one which makes class 2 the more dominant class, a situation which is confirmed when we look at loan words from Latin. The verbs which are borrowed are much more likely to come into class 2 than class 1 (note that only one Latin verb is adopted as a strong verb, namely *scrīfan* 'decree'). Therefore it should not be surprising to realise that the eventual single regular weak verb class, as today, is primarily based on class 2 rather than class 1.

In nouns, the point I want to consider is the shape of the dative plural. When I presented the noun conjugations you may have noted that the dative plural of all nouns had the inflection *-um*. But in later texts, such as Ælfric and after, there is a growing tendency for *-an* to replace *-um*. This is trivial in itself, but of course in the *n*-declension it reduces significantly the degree of inflectional variation which occurs in the plural. This is, therefore, perhaps the first step towards the loss of any variation in the plural of nouns which is one of the marks of Middle English and beyond.

Both these changes are undoubtedly associated with a more general phonological issue. This is that the later the text the more likely it is that unstressed vowels will begin to fall together, so that there can even be a falling together of all the unstressed vowels into something like the **reduced**, or **schwa**, vowel of present-day. Even from a reasonably early date, for example, we can find the plural indicative ending *-on* and the subjunctive ending *-en* falling together as *-en*. This, of course, will promote the loss of a distinctive subjunctive system.

9.3 Prose

The very earliest texts, a mixture of charters, interlinear glosses, that is to say, Latin manuscripts with Old English forms written above the original Latin, and Latin-Old English glossaries, give no real indication of how Old English prose was to develop. Once again we have to wait until the time of Alfred before we find continuous lengthy prose.

The writings of Alfred, or of those who worked beside him, can often seem clumsy to us. The structure of his sentences often consists of a more additive style, clause added to clause without much further subordinate or rhetorical structure. This is undoubtedly unfair, but nevertheless it has more than a grain of truth to it and deserves explanation. It must always be remembered that at that time there was no inherited tradition of formal prose in English. The only models available were Latin prose and, as I shall show shortly, native poetry. The scarcity of stylistic resources accounts for such awkward passages as the following from the earliest, Alfredian, version of the *Anglo-Saxon Chronicle*:

Ond þā onġeat se cyning þæt ond hē on þā duru ēode, ond þā unhēanliċe hine werede oþ hē on þone æþeling lōcude, ond þā ūt ræsde on hine ond hine miċlum ġewundode. Ond hīe alle on þone cyning wærun feohtende oþ þæt hīe hine ofslæġenne hæfdon.

And then the king realised that and went to the door, and then bravely defended himself until he caught sight of the prince, and then he rushed out at him and wounded him severely. And they all started fighting the king until they had slain him

Within a century, however, the situation had changed dramatically. Much of this is due to Ælfric and Wulfstan, both of whose works you have already seen. No doubt both writers brought their own, very different, skills to bear. On the other hand, it is surely noteworthy that they were near contemporaries and, equally, significant players in the Benedictine Monastic Revival which was prominent throughout the second half of the tenth century. It is of little use having skilled writers if there is no educational infrastructure available to permit the exercise of their skills.

I have implied that these writers were different from each other. Indeed, Ælfric was above all a teacher, a private man, whilst Wulfstan was as much a statesman as a monk. This need not detain us here, but it is reflected directly in the type of language they use. As might be expected, both authors are fully acquainted with Latin rhetoric, for example Wulfstan appears to depend greatly on Ciceronian models. But both writers are able to exploit the native structures and vocabulary to permit variation and to leave aside or adjust the Ciceronian style to their own purposes. In the *Sermo Lupi*, for example, you have already seen how native structures, especially, of course, of word formation, are used for rhetorical effect.

There is no space here to examine further the stylistic structures of these writers, except in one particular respect, which will lead us naturally on to the next topic. This is that both writers exploit the structural features most closely identified with Old English poetry. As far as can be determined, this stylistic usage was first invented by Ælfric. The essential features are the use of alliteration and the use of two-stress phrases. Let me give a short example, where I have set the passage out as if it were in lines of Old English poetry so that it appears with two pairs of stress in each line and alliterative syllables in italics (I have, however, removed the normal length marks to avoid clutter):

> Mártinus þa *fér*de to þam *fýr*lenan lánde
> and þa þa he cóm to *mún*tum þa *ġemét*te he *sćéa*ðan
> and heora *án* sóna his *éx*e up abræd
> *wól*de hine sléan ac him for*wýr*nde sum óþer
> swa þæt he þæt *hýl*fe ġelæhte and wið*háf*de þæt sléġe
> Then Martin travelled to a distant land
> and when he came to the mountains he met some robbers
> and one of them immediately raised up his axe
> in order to slay him. But another forewarned him
> so that he caught the handle and restrained the blow

9.4 Poetry

Much more could be said about the prose writers of Old English and especially all three mentioned in the section above, but that would be a distraction here. Yet, as I have said, Ælfric's rhythmical prose is a natural entry point to Old English poetry, itself so linguistically different from the present-day tradition, which owes its origins to the time of Chaucer.

We are used to a metrical system in which the two principal features are a regular pattern of stress and rhyme associated with the final word in a line. The most dominant system is the **iambic pentameter** with its rhyming schemes of the type AABB or ABAB. Obviously there are many variations of this, as, for example, in blank verse, where there is no regular rhyming scheme. Nevertheless we all have the sense that the above principles are the norm.

Therefore it will probably come as a considerable surprise to discover that the iambic pentameter is never used in Old English poetry and that rhyme is sufficiently rare for one poem which does use rhyme to be known today, quite simply, as *The Rhyming Poem*. Since the principles governing Old English poetry are so different from those of the modern tradition, it is worth spending a little time on them.

There were two such guiding principles in Old English: the first concerns stress, as in modern poetry, but the second concerns not rhyme, but rather alliteration. I shall discuss the issue of stress first, but even before I do that, it is necessary to consider what a line of poetry might be. We are so used today to considering poetry as a written medium that it is easy to forget that it is above all an oral medium. To forget that is to forget that it is phonological features such as stress which determine the basic structure or template of the line. Thus an iambic line consists of five feet, in which each foot consists of an unstressed syllable followed by a stressed syllable. Of course poets alter this basic structure (which if it were followed slavishly would be unbearably monotonous), but these deviations are only possible because the template exists.

There was a template in Old English too, of course. It was, however, a very different one. It had two basic features. Firstly, the line consisted of two equal but partially independent parts. We talk of two half-lines forming one long line. Within each half-line there are exactly two fully stressed syllables. It is important to note that the number and position of unstressed syllables is relatively free, the main restriction being that the unstressed syllables should be completely unstressed. This system has not been totally lost from English, for it accords with many traditional nursery-rhymes, for example:

Húmpty Dúmpty sát on a wáll
Húmpty Dúmpty hád a great fáll

Not that Old English poetry is similar to nursery-rhymes, rather it proves that the Old English metrical structures are based on a still-active general template.

I have, in effect, presented in the previous paragraph the stress pattern of Old English poetry. Now I have to add to that the system of alliteration. Alliteration consists of the repetition of the initial sound in either two or three of the stressed syllables of the long line, which we can replicate in present-day English as follows:

> **P**áge's **p**érfect **p**órk sáusages

where I have highlighted in bold the alliterating syllables.

If we examine a real piece of Old English poetry, as in the following examples from the middle of *The Battle of Maldon*, it becomes immediately obvious that the situation is much more complex than I have so far indicated:

1	Féoll þa to fóldan	féalohilte swúrd:
	fell then to ground	yellow-hilted sword
2	ne míhte he ġehéaldan	héardne méċe
	not could he hold	hard blade
3	wǽpnes wéaldan.	þa ġyt þæt wórd ġecwǽð
	weapon wield	Then yet the word spoke
4	hár hílderinc	hýssan býlde
	hoary battle-warrior	warriors encouraged
5	bǽd gángan forð	góde ġeféran
	urged go forward	brave companions

At first sight it appears hard to make sense of the patterns which occur here. But there is method, nevertheless. Taking each half-line as a separate entity, it should be possible to observe that lines 1a, 2b, 3a, 4b and 5b (where 'a' and 'b' refer to the first or second half-line respectively) have a common structure, namely they have an initial stressed syllable followed by one or more unstressed syllables. Let us call this the falling-falling type, or type A.

In fact there appears to have been five types of half-line. In addition to the falling-falling type A, there was rising-rising type B, clashing type C, broken-fall type D and fall-and-rise type E. In the short extract above, naturally, not all types appear. But of the other five half-lines beyond the five mentioned above, we find the following. 1a is type E, where there is secondary stress on the compound *féalohìlte*; 3b is type B with, as you can see, several unstressed syllables preceding the first stressed syllable; 4a is an example of D with an unstressed syllable 'breaking' the second stressed syllable from the secondary stress of the compound, i.e. *hílderìnc*; the same holds for 5a, where *forð* is a separable prefix.

Before I continue, it might serve as a useful guide if I now present a schematic representation of the above types, which were first presented at the end of the nineteenth century by Eduard Sievers (see the recommended reading). Essentially these types consist of a pattern of fully stressed (/), partly stressed (i.e. with secondary stress) (\) and fully unstressed (x) syllables. The number of unstressed syllables is relatively unimportant; indeed, in Old Saxon poetry they can occur very extensively indeed. To the little sketch below, therefore, you can add extra unstressed syllables after the unstressed syllables given there. Here are the five types of half-line:

A   / x / x
B   x / x /
C   x / / x
D   / / \ x
E   / \ x /

You may have noticed that in the extract above there is still one half-line unaccounted for, namely 2a: *ne míhte he gehéaldan*, and equally it appears to be unaccounted for in the five schematic types. If I say that this half-line is a type A (falling-falling type), the obvious problem is that there is an initial unstressed syllable to explain. Such an initial syllable is quite often found and indeed is a part of general metrical theory, not particular to Old English. It is usually referred to as **anacrusis**. It occurs far more often in type A half-lines than anywhere else, for reasons you should be able to work out yourself.

There are several other variations which can occur, and of these perhaps the one that must be noted here can be found in the following half-line:

héofona hláford

There is a metrical requirement that every stressed syllable must be heavy (see the discussion in Chapter 3 for how this operates). This poses no problem in the case of *hláford*, where the stressed syllable is indeed heavy. However, it is clear that the stressed syllable of *heofona* is light, for its diphthong is short and there is only a single following consonant. The metrical rule which saves such forms is called **resolution**. Resolution states that a light syllable occupies a stressed position if the immediately following syllable is also light. This is phonologically parallel to the morphological position where, as shown in Chapter 3, heavy-stemmed *word* 'words' is the equivalent of light-stemmed *scipu* 'ships'.

If we now turn to the system of alliteration, there are several interesting features which in part reflect interestingly on the present-day language. Essentially, as the example above from *The Battle of Maldon* shows, alliteration links two or three stressed syllables in the long line in terms of identical initial consonants. This itself demonstrates that alliteration has a stylistic and functional meaning not dissimilar to rhyme in later poetry. There are still questions to be asked, however, notably, which syllables alliterate, how many syllables alliterate, and which sounds count as identical?

Usually alliteration is based on the first stressed syllable of the second half-line and the initial consonant of that syllable must alliterate with the stronger of the two stressed syllables in the first half-line. I cannot here go into the vexed question of how we determine which syllable that might be, but roughly speaking nouns, adjectives, infinitives and participles are stronger than verbs and adverbs. The other stressed syllable of the first half-line may, however, participate in the alliteration also. The same, however, is not true of the second stressed syllable of the second half-line, which can only participate in alliteration in very special circumstances which are outside the scope of this work. There are exceptions to the above, but they are mostly a matter of literary style, and do not affect the fundamental linguistic points.

I still have to address the question of which sounds count as identical. The essential position is that only one single consonant is involved in the alliteration. But that leaves three cases to consider. Firstly, it is normally the case that if there is an initial consonant cluster, then alliteration still remains associated with only the initial consonant, as can be seen in another line from the same poem as before:

| bræd of þam beorne | blódiġe gár |
| dragged from the warrior | bloody spear |

However, if the initial cluster is either *sc-*, *sp-* or *st-*, then that cluster alliterates only with itself, as can be seen in two further lines from the same poem:

he sċéaft þa mid ðam sċýlde	þat se sċeaft tobærst
he thrust then with the shield	so the shaft broke
and þæt spére sprengde	þæt hit sprang ongéan
and the spear broke	so that it sprang back

This has interesting parallels with present-day English, where /s/ + voiceless stop clusters have a special status. There is good reason for supposing that in both Old English and in present-day English the initial sequence /s/ + voiceless stop function as an indivisible unit, and not merely in alliteration, but in general matters such as determining the internal structure of syllables.

In contrast to the above, alliteration between vowels appears to have no constraints, so that any vowel alliterates with any other vowel:

ǽtterne órd	Se éorl wæs þe blíþra
poisoned point	The earl was the happier

This situation has caused much controversy. The dominant view is that things were simply as they appear on the surface, but another view is that there was something preceding the apparently alliterating vowel. The only plausible something is a glottal stop, as is found medially in non-standard pronunciations of, say, *bitter*, which, of course, the Old English scribes would have no way of representing. Of course this also means we have no direct data to allow us to prove that this the correct view. No doubt the controversy will persist. One argument in favour of positing an initial glottal stop is that such a sound is indeed found in Dutch and German. I have to say that I remain unconvinced, but you should make up your own mind!

The final point to consider takes us back to another question about what sounds count as identical. Here are two different examples from *Beowulf*:

ġéong in ġéardum	þone Gód sénde
child in years	that God sent
ćéasterbúendum	cénra ġehwýlcum
fortress-dwellers	brave ones every

At first sight it might not be obvious that there is a problem in these two lines. Closer examination, however, shows that the alliteration between /j/ (<ġ>) and /g/ (<g>) is between two different phonemes, which are by definition non-identical. One possibility is that we are dealing with eye-alliteration, that is to say, the alliteration is only graphic, a matter of how the alliteration is presented on paper (or, rather, on vellum manuscript). But that is scarcely possible, both in terms of literacy and the fundamentally oral nature of Old English poetry. It is far more probable that it reflects an earlier historical state when distinctive palatal phonemes did not exist.

9.5 Dialect

The final issue I want to discuss concerns dialects. So far all the texts we have considered, with one special exception which I shall raise shortly, are from one form or another of West Saxon, as I mentioned in Chapter 1. This is unavoidable in a work such as this, especially given that perhaps as much as ninety per cent of the textual material from the period has come down to us in such a form. Even, and this is the exception I mentioned above, the poetry is virtually all contained in four West Saxon-based manuscripts, although there is a great deal of internal evidence that much of it was originally composed in a more northerly dialect. This certainly true of *Beowulf.* But there are pressing reasons why, even in an introductory work such as this, the other dialects cannot be ignored.

One reason is not really to do with Old English as such but is instead a matter of understanding the development of the history of English as a whole. For after the Norman Conquest and the disappearance of English from sight, it of course remained the language of all but an aristocratic elite. And when it re-emerged, the political centres of power had shifted, in the language as elsewhere. West Saxon was no longer a cultural dominance. Rather, it was other dialects, especially those around London and the East Midlands, which were to have the strongest influence on what forms of English were to prevail in later centuries. It is, therefore, important to have some understanding of where the other Old English dialects fit into the overall scheme of things.

There are, as I suggested in Chapter 1, considerable difficulties in assessing the dialect situation in Old English. The standard view has been that there were four dialect areas: West Saxon, Kentish, Mercian and Northumbrian. West Saxon, of course, had its centre in Winchester and the surrounding Thames Valley area. However, especially after the establishment of the Danelaw to the north and east, the efforts of Alfred the Great to create a unified kingdom, and the eventual success of Alfred's efforts, the influence of West Saxon gradually spread, both to the south-east, including London, and across to the Severn Valley.

The most immediate effect was on Kentish, with its major monasteries, especially, but not only, at Canterbury. Thus, whilst we have a number of valuable texts from Kentish, only those written up to about 900 demonstrate a form of the language that is more or less distinctively Kentish. From then on we find either texts which are most West Saxon-like or which show a mixture of Kentish and other more general southern, and West Saxon, traces. For a clearer picture of the south-east we have to wait until the evidence from Middle English begins to arrive, around 1200.

I want next to consider Northumbrian, which is perhaps the simplest of all the dialects to contextualise. Although Northumbria itself covers a huge area, from about Edinburgh down to the Humber and from Carlisle down to the Mersey, the texts we have all come from a tiny area centring on the major ecclesiastical centre at Durham. This must be remembered. There is some evidence that a few texts display a slightly more southerly origin, but if this is so we cannot tell exactly where that might be, even if our suspicions focus on York.

Northumbrian is of particular interest because the majority of texts, of which the best known is *The Lindisfarne Gospels*, a perfectly beautiful manuscript only spoiled, luckily for us, by a scratched Old English gloss written above the lines of the original Latin text, show the first signs of both Viking influence and the disappearance of several features, particularly morphological, which belong to Old English but which are to be lost in the later development of the language.

For example, where most more southerly texts, especially West Saxon, use the form *synd* 'are' or variants of that, Northumbrian frequently uses *aron*, the source of the present-day form. In the noun, Northumbrian often shows a falling together of various determiner forms which has sometimes led to the belief that the system of grammatical gender (most obviously supplied by unambiguous determiners) was being lost. This is probably not true, or at least over-presumptive, but rather there is a new development occurring which will dynamically interact with the loss of gender on other grounds, including the frequent interchangeability of all unstressed vowels in these texts. It is the conjunction of all these different effects which eventually lead to the loss of grammatical gender in Middle English.

But it is Mercian which causes the greatest number of difficulties in terms of dialect. This, of course, is unfortunate, since from the point of view of later developments it would be nice if we could draw a straight line from Old English down to, say 1400, the time of Chaucer. No such line, however, is available. Moreover, although there is a tendency to see Mercian as the dialect of the area between the Mersey and the Humber in the north and the Thames in the south, this is quite misleading, for at least two reasons.

Firstly, it ignores the fact that we have no useful material from East Anglia, which plays a critical role in later developments. And, secondly, it ignores the geographical distribution of the material we do have. For given the area which Mercia might be held to cover, the actual texts we have come from a rather restricted area. The best-known text, *The Vespasian Psalter*, almost certainly comes from the Lichfield area, about twenty-five miles north-east of Birmingham. Another important text, *The Rushworth Gospels*, which was once thought to come from Yorkshire (outside the traditional Mercian area) is now more plausibly placed near Lichfield too. This is no peculiarity, since Lichfield was both the home of the Mercian leaders and a major ecclesiastical centre. Other texts which we have appear to come from areas perhaps just to the east of the Severn Valley. Thus we lack any substantial evidence about the whole of the

East Midlands, just the area we might be most interested in. The only evidence we have for that area is from place-names and rare charters, rather less material in all than we have for, say, Kentish.

Many of the features which distinguish this 'Lichfield Mercian', as it might be called, from the other principal dialects, in particular West Saxon, look individually to be matters of detail, but they cover all levels of the language. In phonology there is the raising of the short vowel /æ/ to a new phoneme /ɛ/, in morphology there are distinctive inflexions, such as -u, not -e for the 1st person present indicative singular (this is shared with Northumbrian and, partially, Kentish), in syntax the process of negative contraction (see §7.5) is less frequently employed.

Beyond these details, however, there is an overarching feature. This is that, from probably a rather early date, certainly by 800 or so, a distinct Mercian literary language was developing long before any such dialect appeared in West Saxon. The text which best expresses this is the ninth-century *Vespasian Psalter*. It continues to be found in texts written just after the Conquest, notably a text called *The Life of St Chad*, a tenth-century bishop of Lichfield.

This is of importance because there has been a strong tendency for Late West Saxon to be viewed as a kind of Standard Old English. But Lichfield Mercian has every right to be seen as an equal to Late West Saxon, and that rather implies that there was no Standard Old English, but rather at least two varieties which are best described as **focussed**. That is to say, they were both varieties which speakers tended to favour, rather than fixed standard languages to which speakers were required to adhere, by, for example, prescribed educational standards.

Exercise

The exercise in this chapter is designed to bring together the two central topics which I have discussed here, namely poetry and dialects. In the first part below, therefore, I have given you a complete short poem which you should attempt to analyse metrically, i.e. work out the stress patterns of each half-line and also determine the alliterative pattern of each long line. The poem I have chosen is *Cædmon's Hymn*. You have already trans-lated some aspect of the story of Cædmon, so you can now see his art.

Nū sculon heriġean	heofonrīċes Weard,
Meotodes meahte	ond his mōdġeþanc,
weorc Wuldorfæder,	swā hē wundra ġehwæs,
ēċe Drihten	ōr onstealde.
Hē ærest sċeōp	eorðan bearnum

heofon tō hrōfe,	hālig Sċyppend.
þā middangeard	monncynnes Weard
ēċe Drihten	æfter tēode
fīrum foldan,	Frēa ælmihtig.

Unusually, but not uniquely, there is another version of this poem extant, which is written in the Northumbrian dialect. Indeed, there are four Northumbrian versions, for any work that was widely admired was often copied several, and occasionally, as with Ælfric's work, many times; the unusualness I refer to lies in the work appearing in markedly different dialects. Of the Northumbrian versions, the earliest version is called the Moore version, which was written in 737, probably fewer than seventy-five years after Cædmon's own death, whilst another version, Leningrad, was written in 746, both within fifteen years of Bede's death. Here is the Moore version:

Nū sċylun hergan	hefænrīċaes Uard,
Metudæs maecti	end his mōdgidanc,
uerc Uuldurfadur,	suē hē uundra gihuaes,
ēċi Dryctin	ōr āstelidæ.
Hē āērist sċōp	aelda barnum
heben til hrōfe,	hāleg Sċepen.
Thā middungeard	moncynnaes Uard,
ēċi Dryctin	æfter tīadæ
fīrum foldu	Frēa allmectig.

At this stage you do not, of course, have sufficient knowledge to attempt a detailed dialectal comparison. But it should be possible for you to attempt to compare the two texts in other ways. For example, are there any major contrasts between them? What differences can be explained solely because there are differences in spelling-systems? If you assume, correctly, that unstressed front vowels fall together as /e/ in the later text, can you find examples to demonstrate that? One important point to note here is that as well as geographical distinction, there can also be distinctions of date. The West Saxon text belongs to the first half of the tenth century. Given the questions I pose above, might some of the above contrasts be due to a difference of approximately 200 years between the two versions?

10 The future

10.1 Introduction

But first the past. In the preceding chapters I have attempted to give you an overview of the principal characteristics of Old English. In doing this the concentration has been on the areas of morphology, syntax and vocabulary. By now you should have a good grasp of the fundamental issues in these areas. Although I have occasionally touched on phonological issues, I have tried to avoid these as much as possible, believing that they are best tackled later. If you wish to study Old English in more detail, that will be one of your first tasks.

In morphology, you have learned about the structure of nouns, adjectives and verbs. In nouns you have seen the major declensional classes and the features of these classes which are, to a greater or lesser extent, no longer present in English, in particular the concepts of case and grammatical gender. In adjectives perhaps the most surprising feature was the syntactically determined 'declension' of adjectives, a feature entirely absent from the present-day language. Two features, perhaps, stand out in respect of verbs. First of all we explored the basic differences between weak and strong verbs and introduced the concept of Ablaut, which, although it remains as a relic today, is no longer synchronically active. Secondly we explored the variations in tense and mood which are rather different in Old English from those usages today.

In syntax, of course, it was necessary to start with a discussion of how some of the morphological patterns were realised in practice. This meant that we had to discuss, for example, how case was employed and for what purposes it was used. And the same is true for other features, too, such as, once more, tense and mood. But you were also able to understand several other important differences between Old English and present-day English. Probably the most important of these is the issue of word-order, for what you saw was that the basic word system of Old English involved two rival orders. In main clauses the verb usually occupied second position in the clause, whereas in subordinate clauses the verb usually occupied final position. Both of these, in different ways, contrast with the strict SVO word order today. You also saw that there were other features which were quite noticeably different from anything today, such as the use of negation and impersonal verbs. Relative clauses, too, had their own distinctive traits.

The feeling that 'older' languages must be somehow more primitive than languages today is one that has a quite general currency, even if not amongst linguists. This feeling can even be exaggerated by the history of English where, over the last 1000 years, there has been an enormous growth in vocabulary, and in particular in the huge number of loan words from an almost incredible range of languages. In Old English, as you have seen, there were very few loan words, and the majority were taken from Latin, no doubt partly due to the conversion of the English to Christianity, but also partly because so many of our texts are derived from the work of monastic writers fluent in Latin. But the measurement of a language's vitality is not adequately measured by the degree to which it is indebted to other languages! And what you have seen is that Old English had a wealth of internal resources of its own with which to create new vocabulary. The most obvious resource was compounding, as exemplified above all by the poetry, but there was also a very frequent and widespread use of affixation.

10.2 The past

In understanding Old English, as you have seen, it is essential to have some knowledge of what happened before Old English. One of the very first points made in Chapter 1 was that Old English ultimately derives from Indo-European, a hypothetical language which perhaps existed about 10,000 years ago. And, less distantly, Old English derived from Germanic, itself a hypothetical descendant from Indo-European which existed in the centuries before and after the time of Christ. I introduced these languages because they explain so much about why Old English looks as it does.

This need to look at the past is one which you too should now be able to recognise. For example, the word order system of Old English is not only shared with other Germanic languages of the time, but is also discernibly related to other older Indo-European languages, such as Latin. The system of declension and the allied markers of gender and case can be traced back to a system which must have operated in Indo-European. The strong verb system and the whole Ablaut phenomenon is also something which has its origins in Indo-European, although it was drastically re-organised in the evolution of Germanic, so that the strong verbs now look a basically Germanic feature. These latter features, the development of strong and weak verbs and the radical restructuring of Ablaut, also contribute greatly, although it is often difficult to see, to the creation of Old English vocabulary.

There are other, perhaps less expected, features which owe their origins to a much earlier state. This is the case with, for example, Old English poetry. It is known, for instance, that there is continental poetry, especially from Old Saxon, which shares the distinctive features of Old English poetry. We also know that Scandinavian poetry not only had some of these features too but also used particular processes of compounding which help to explain the so-frequent use of compounds in Old English poetry. And this must be a shared inheritance, given the antiquity of both traditions. Furthermore, given that in origin Old English poetry is likely to have been oral in nature (see again the story of Cædmon), it should also be noted that oral poetry of this kind can be found in, for example, many areas of the Balkans and Greece (recall here the poetry of Homer), where it may even still survive. That looks like a common, if much altered, feature which may have been widespread amongst the speakers of many of the Indo-European languages.

10.3 Towards Middle English and beyond

I have already pointed out signs that the structures of Old English were open to change. In Chapter 9 you saw some evidence for that in the brief discussion of verb morphology and gender. But that is scarcely even the tip of the iceberg. And there is always the question of how it can be that there is so great a disjunction between the structures of Old English and those of the present-day language. Certainly there is no inevitability about it. This can quite easily be seen by comparing any of the stages of English with those of, say, German. In comparative terms, German has hardly changed at all; it remains a clearly Germanic (as opposed to a German!) language, retaining many of the features which it shared with and which you have seen in Old English. This puzzle of the huge changes in English means that one question which sensibly can be, and has been, asked is whether present-day English is really a Germanic language at all.

Some of the issues here lie more properly in the scope of the companion book on Middle English in the same series as this. Nevertheless it is useful to take a look at these issues from the Old English perspective rather than merely to look back. That can have the danger of turning Old English into an outsider, as not really an integral part of the cultural as well as the linguistic story of the English-speaking world. It is only by examining the structural and cultural history of Old English that we can hope to see how it fits into the history of English as a whole. In addition this will help us to understand more about present-day English and how English has come to be as it is.

Many of the problems are falsely explained as the result of the Norman Conquest. This is not to deny the cultural importance of the Norman Conquest, but linguistically its effects began to loom large only in the later parts of the thirteenth century and even then they were dominant only in the area of vocabulary. The Viking invasions almost certainly had a more widespread influence over many areas of the language, and we have seen some of this already. But even Viking influence was restricted, this time geographically, to the north and east. More important than either of these influences were the inherent long-term structural issues. It is to these that we must now look, for if they had not already existed, then the effects of both the Viking invasions and the coming of the Normans would both have fallen on stony ground. Nevertheless I shall return to these issues of language contact shortly.

I have already mentioned, in Chapter 9, one relevant point, namely the falling together of the unstressed vowels. But this falling together, which itself was to herald their widespread loss, is not enough to explain the upsets which occurred in, for example, the declensional systems. To see what might happen, however, let us take another look at noun declensions. In Old English there were, as I first discussed in Chapter 2, three major declensions, alongside a variety of minor declensions. These were the General Masculine, the General Feminine and the N-declensions. I know this ignores the General Neuter, but I have already shown that this is close in structure to the general masculines and therefore I shall silently include it there. Typical examples of each declension are repeated below for ease, where I have changed the typical noun for the *n*-declension by choosing a noun current today:

Masculine	*Singular*	*Plural*
Nominative	stān	stānas
Accusative	stān	stānas
Genitive	stānes	stāna
Dative	stāne	stānum

Feminine	*Singular*	*Plural*
Nom.	talu	tala
Acc.	tale	tala
Gen.	tale	tala
Dat.	tale	talum

N-	*Singular*	*Plural*
Nom.	nama	naman
Acc.	naman	naman
Gen.	naman	namena
Dat.	naman	namum

Let us now see what happens if we assume that every unstressed vowel becomes reduced to something like schwa. You may also recall that in Chapter 9 I suggested that the dative plural ending had already started to develop as *-an* rather than *-um*. Taking these two points together, it is quite easy to see that both the feminine declension and the *n*-declension suffer disproportionately badly. The former will no longer have any distinctive inflexions, not even in terms of number, except in the dative plural. But there, of course, every declension will have the same inflection because of the spread of *-an*. The *n*-declension will retain a distinction between nominative singular and nominative plural, but every other distinction except the marginal genitive plural will have gone. On the other hand, the masculine declension remains relatively intact, since the final *-s* is preserved, both in the genitive singular and the nominative-accusative plural.

The consequences of this are highly significant. Since this means that the feminines and the *n*-nouns no longer have any helpful inflectional markers, there is quickly a shift in most, but not all, areas of the country to a single major declension, based on the historical masculine declension. Furthermore, there are other phonological developments which cause the loss of final *-n*, a process already well underway in Northumbria in the Old English period itself and which is partly, although somewhat obscured, reflected in the form *foldu* in the Northumbrian text at the end of Chapter 9; it comes from an earlier form *foldun*. At a later stage still, although still in the early part of the Middle English period, there is a process by which short stressed vowels are lengthened when followed by a single consonant.

We can take as an example the following changes in the nominative singular and plural of the Old English noun *nama*:

nama   → namə   → namə   → naːmə   → naːm
naman   → namən   → namə   → naːmə   → naːm

That exemplification is a dramatic demonstration of why such nouns become associated with the masculine declension and why that declension is now the only regular declension in English. That, in other words, is why we now have the plural *names*. Obviously present-day English has a number of exceptions, such as the retention of the *n*-declension in *oxen*, and there may be even more examples in various dialects, for example *shoon* 'shoes' in Scots. There are other unusual developments too, such as the shift to Ø-plurals of some animal names, for example *sheep*, which is an innovation but based on a transfer to the general neuter declension.

To think that the above discussion, however interesting, is all there is to say here would be a mistake. The repercussions, or interactions, go well beyond the matter of noun declensions. The most important place to look in order to gauge the extent of the overall changes in English is to be found in the changes which are about to take place in word order. Let us, therefore, turn to this subject and the interaction between those changes and the declensional changes.

The essential point about word order in Old English which we have to take into account is that during the period there was a general rise in the proportion of clauses with verb-second word order. There is considerable argument about how this might have occurred. There is perhaps some agreement that several different factors were at work. These may have included the preference for light elements to appear at the beginning of clauses and, correspondingly, for heavy elements to appear towards the end; allied to this is an increasing preference for relative clauses to appear to the right of the whole clause containing the antecedent; and a further point may be the increasing preference to place the object after the whole verb structure rather than after the first verb in the group.

These issues were raised in Chapter 7, but it is noteworthy that in a text of the mid-twelfth century, namely *The Peterborough Chronicle*, the dominance of verb-second structure is considerable and clearly the move to the strict SVO order of present-day English is beginning to be possible. To what extent is the shift due, not to the points raised in the previous paragraph, but rather to the loss of inflections in nouns (and perhaps also, but there is no space to argue this here, in verbs)? Clearly, the loss of distinctive noun inflections, in particular the loss of nominative ~ accusative ~ dative distinctions so that only number and genitive inflections remain, as in present-day English, is significant.

So at first sight we could argue that the loss of inflections is paramount. It is certainly true that the loss of inflections makes it more difficult to distinguish between subjects and objects and, indeed, indirect objects. In the latter case it is noticeable that at the end of Old English period there is a greater use of prepositions, a further indication of the ongoing structural changes in the language. In the former case, however, it should be noted that pronouns retain the distinctive nominative ~ accusative forms. There can be no doubt that the loss of inflections is part of the overall picture, but it would still be rather rash to assume that this was the defining cause of the word order changes.

Firstly, it has to be noted that several of the changes, as described above, were already under way before the loss of declensional structure caused the loss of unstressed vowels. Secondly, the placement of light and heavy elements was undoubtedly entirely independent of the situation in unstressed syllables. Thirdly, it is noticeable that in closely related languages where, for example, case marking also becomes vestigial, as happens, albeit at a much later stage, in Dutch, word order changes, although clearly observable, do not result in the strict SVO order found in present-day English. Even in a somewhat more remote, in structural terms, language such as French, note how object pronouns precede their verb, even although noun objects follow their verb. This neatly leads us to the next point.

An alternative view, which I explored earlier in this chapter, namely that the changes are due to the Viking and Norman invasions, is all the more unlikely in light of the further discussion. Everything we have seen points to the various changes having germinated in English before the influence of either invading group had made itself felt. It would be foolish to deny such influences, but they have to be seen for what they produced.

Viking influence was to be in many ways more influential in core areas of the language than French, and may therefore have promoted the changes we have been discussing. Thus we owe to the Scandinavian languages not only the verb form *are*, already mentioned, but also key items in the pronoun system, such as *they*, which replaces the Old English pronoun *hī*. The Old English prepositional system too was significantly modified with some pronouns, such as *æt* 'at' and *wið* 'with' receiving additional meaning and more prominence.

Such cases, however, are probably merely symptomatic, for it is the overall situation which is crucial. Throughout the north and the east, the area of the Danelaw, there must have been many Anglo-Viking communities comprised of both English and Danish or Norwegian speakers. In such a situation, where the languages were so similar, there must have been considerable language contact, perhaps resulting in something of a creole situation. This would result in, amongst other things, a simplification of grammatical structures. Such simplification would interact with the changing structures of English and emphasise them.

This is rather confirmed by the effects of Norman French. Although we often think that French, of whatever variety, caused most of the major changes in English, in fact the influence of French was much more restricted. The greatest impact of French was undoubtedly, and remains, on vocabulary. To some extent this may have occurred because the Old English methods of word-formation were being lost in any case. However, it also caused the creation of new vocabulary alongside the old, and to some extent this is still reflected today; compare, for example, *kingly* from OE *cyningliċe* and *royal* from French. In other areas, however, and especially in syntax and morphology, there was only a small effect. The changing nature of Old English phonology, on the other hand, when combined with the influx of French loans, probably contributed to the introduction of French stress systems, particularly in respect of poly-syllabic items. But compared with Scandinavian, there appears to have been significantly less bilingualism, and this, together with the very different nature of French linguistic structure, inhibited the possibility of any similar creole situation arising. Furthermore, the fact that French only significantly affected English after the period of the changes we have discussed were fully under way or even complete, makes the influence of French on core elements of structure less probable.

10.4 Envoi

Perhaps, rather than this French word, you would have preferred me to use the French-Latin loan *conclusion*. I doubt very much that you would have been impressed if I had used the Old English word *ending* (OE *endung*). This is, of course, a matter of style and **register**, or the different varieties of language available to speakers. And as such it serves as a reminder that we can never have access to all the varieties of English before the Norman Conquest.

But even accepting this lack, it remains the case that Old English is the foundation of the present-day language. As we have just seen, neither the Viking nor the Norman invasions by themselves created the language we have today. For this reason alone, the study of Old English is essential for an understanding of the language in which you are reading this text.

English arrived in Britain as the language of invaders, a language which at the time was not clearly distinct from the other languages of the North Sea coast and its hinterland. Within no more than two centuries it had banished to the periphery the Celtic languages spoken by those it invaded. One of my principal aims, therefore, has been to demonstrate this Germanic inheritance. By now, therefore, you should have an under-standing of the principal Germanic features, such as the noun, adjective and verbal morphology, the word order system and the methods of word formation. However I have also attempted to demonstrate, especially in the later stages of this book, how such structures were able to develop into the language of today.

In the section on recommended reading below, I make a number of suggestions which will enable you to further your study of both Old English and its later developments. One point which needs to be made here, however, is the following. In order to understand and, even more so, to evaluate the material which I have presented above, it is necessary to read texts written in Old English. Only in this way will you be able to recognise the patterns of the language.

Exercises

Just as at the halfway stage of this book I presented you with a set of questions which might allow you to assess and present the material you had seen, so here I present you with a set of essay questions one or more of which you might like to attempt. There is a reasonable amount of choice here, so I shall make some suggestions about each.

1. Is English a Germanic language?

You can answer this question in two ways. You could start from Old English and then show some aspects which have either changed or remained. Or you could start from present-day English and work backwards.

2. What are the sources of Old English vocabulary?

It is important to remember that this includes the original vocabulary, as well as word-formation strategies and borrowing.

3. To what extent does Old English vocabulary contribute to the vocabulary of the present-day language?

This is the opposite question to (2). Now you have to assess the extent to which Old English vocabulary, including its processes of word formation, forms the core of the present-day vocabulary.

4. Write an essay on Old English word order, using examples from the texts which have been presented.

The point of this essay is not merely for you to write a standard essay on the topic. If you use a good range of examples, then you will discover that Old English word order is rather more complex than my summary descriptions have suggested.

5. Analyse the structure of Old English strong verbs and compare that structure with that of such verbs in the present-day language.

This is a difficult topic, and depends as much on your knowledge of the present-day language as on Old English. But the hope is that you will be able to discern how much of the Old English verb system has remained and how much has been lost.

6. Explain the metrical system of most Old English poetry and consider also the use of poetic vocabulary.

Here you will need to read considerably more poetry than I have presented. However, a poem such as *The Wanderer* will be a useful start. You should provide an analysis of a range of stress patterns and also interesting examples of alliteration. In terms of vocabulary, pay especial attention to the use of compounds.

Old English – present-day English glossary

Nouns are indicated by their gender and, in the case of *n*-declension nouns only, by their declension. Nouns which occur only in the plural are marked 'plural'. Verbs are indicated by their class membership, i.e. 1, 2, I, II, etc. Irregular verbs are indicated by 'anom' and preterite-present verbs by 'pr-pr'. Strong verbs which have a weak present tense are marked 'wk pr'. Other contractions are: adj = adjective, advb = adverb, conj = conjunction, dem = demonstrative, prep = preposition, pron = pronoun.

ā advb	always
abbudisse f	abbess
abrēoðan II	fall away
aflēoġan I	defeat
āġen adj	own
ān num	one, a certain
anbīdian 2	await
and, ond conj	and
andweard adj	present
anforlǣtan VII	renounce
Antecrīst m	Antichrist
apostata m(n)	apostate
āðbrīce m	perjury
ǣfre advb	ever
ǣfter prep	after, in search of
ǣġhwǣr advb	everywhere
ǣġðer ge conj	both … and
ælde m (plural)	men
ælmihtiġ adj	almighty
ǣr advb	previously
ǣr prep	before
ǣrest advb	firstly
ǣrne morġen adj + n	early morning
ǣswiċ m	oath-breaking

æt prep	at
ǣwbryċe m	adultery
ǣġðer ge conj	both ... and
ǣġhwǣr advb	everywhere
bēodan II	offer
bēon anom	be
bearn n	child
becuman III	come
befrīnan I	inquire
beheonan prep	this side of
besittan V (wk pr)	harass
besmītan I	defile
biddan V (wk pr)	pray
binnan prep	inside
bisċeop m	bishop
blætsian 2	bless
boda m(n)	messenger
bōt f	remedy
brōðor m	brother
bunda m(n)	householder
burhmann m	citizen
burġ f	town
ġebyrian 2	pertain
byrne f(n)	corslet
cēosan II	choose
clǣne adj	clean
clyppan 1	accept
ġecnawan VII	know
crīsten adj	christian
cuman V	come
cweðan V	say
cyng see cyning	
cyning m	king
ċyriċhata m(n)	church-hater
dǣd f	deed
dǣl m	part
dæġ m	day
dæġhwamliċe advb	daily
dēofol n	devil
dōn anom	do
drihten m	lord
dwelian 2	lead astray

dysiġ adj   foolish

ēa f	river
ēac advb	also
eall advb	all
ēast advb	eastwards
ēċe adj	eternal
eft advb	again
ende m	end
eodorcan 1	chew cud
eorðe f(n)	earth
etan V	eat
eġesliċ adj	terrible

fēran 1	go
fæstenbryċe m	non-observance of fasts
faran VI	go
fela adj	many
feorrian 2	go away
ġefera m(n)	comrade
fīras m (plural)	men
flēon II	flee
folc n	people
folde f(n)	earth
for prep	for, because of
forlēogan II	lie
forlēosan II	lose
forliger n	fornication
forloren see forlēosan	
foroft advb	very often
forsyngian 2	sin greatly
frēa m	lord
frēolsbriċe m	non-observance of church festivals
fram prep	from
ful advb	full
ful n	cup
fultum m	help

ġear n	year
ġelome see -lome	
ġeond prep	throughout
ġeong adj.	young
ġeorne advb	eagerly, well
ġīferness f	greed
ġifu f	grace

ġītsung f	avarice
ġynd see ġeond	
gōd n	goods
god m	god, God
godcund adj	divine
grim adj	cruel
grimliċ adj	cruel

hādbryċe m	priest-killing
hāliġ adj	holy
hāmweard advb	homewards
hātan VII	order
hǣðen adj	heathen
he pron	he
healf adj	half
ġehelpan III	help
hēo pron	she
heofon m	heaven
heofonrīċ n	kingdom of heaven
heorð m	hearth
hēr advb	here
herian 1	praise
heriġean see herian	
hetol adj	hostile
hī, hȳ pron	they
hihtan 1	rejoice
hit pron	it
hlāf m	bread
hōcorwyrde adj	derisive
hrōf m	roof
hū advb	how
huru advb	indeed
hūs n	house
hūsbunda m(n)	householder
hwā pron	who, what
ġehwā adj	every, each
ġehwǣs see ġehwa	
hwæt see hwā	
ġehwerfan 1	turn
ġehyran 1	hear
ġehyrnes f	hearing

iċ pronI	
īċan 1	increase
īhte see īcan	

innian 2	lodge (in an inn)
is see bēon	
lagu f	law
lahbryċe m	law-breaking
lang adj	long
lāreow m	teacher
lǣran 1	instruct
lǣttewestre f(n)	guide
lēasung f	lying
lēodhata m(n)	tyrant
lēof adj	dear
leornian 2	learn
lēoð n	song
ġelician 2	like
līf n	life
ġelome advb	frequently
lufian 2	love
lytel adj	little
mā advb	more
magan pr-pr	can
mandǣd f	crime
maneġe see maniġ	
manfull adj	wicked
maniġ adj	many
mann m	man
mannsylen f	slavery
manslyht m	manslaughter
māre adj	more
martyr m	martyr
mæniġfeald adj	manifold
mæġ m	kinsman
mæġ see magan	
mǣġrǣs m	attacking kinsmen
meaht f	power
metod m	creator
mid prep	with
middanġeard m	world
mīl f	mile
misdǣd f	misdeed
mislimpan III	go wrong
mistliċ adj	various
mōdġeðanc m	thought
monian 2	urge

monncynn n	mankind
morðdǣd f	murder
mūð m	mouth
munuchād m	monastic life
ǧemyndgian 2	remember
mynster n	monastery

nā advb	not
nān neg, see ān	
nǣfre advb	never
nǣron neg, see wesan	
nǣs neg, see wesan	
ne advb	not
nēalǣċan 1	approach
nēten n	cattle
niht f	night
nis neg, see bēon	
nū advb	now
nystan neg, see witan	
nȳd f	necessity

ofer prep	over
oferhoga m(n)	despiser
ofslēan VI	slay
ofslōg see ofslēan	
ofst n	haste
oft advb	often
on prep	in
ondrincan III	drink up
onfōn VII	accept
onginnan III	begin
onstellan 2	establish
ōr n	beginning
oð prep	until
ōðer adj, pron	other
oððe conj	or

rǣd m	advice
rǣran 1	rise up
reċċan 1	care
ǧerestan 1	stay
ricsian 2	rule
riht n	justice
ǧerihtan 1	direct
rihtlagu f	just law

sǣ f	sea
ġesċeadwis adj	discreet
sċeal pr-pr	shall, must
sċēop see sċyppan	
scolde see sċeal	
sċulon see sċeal	
sċyppan VI (wk pr)	create
sċyppend m	creator
searacræft m	fraud
self pron, adj	self
sēo see se	
se þæt sēo pron (dem)	that, the
seolf see self	
sibleġer n	incest
simle, symle advb	always
smēan 2	consider
snǣdan 1	eat a meal
ġesomnung f	company
sōna advb	immediately
song m	song
sōð adj	true
specan see sprecan	
spell n	message
sprecan V	speak
stalu f	theft
stǣr n	story
strūdung f	robbery
sum pron, adj	a certain, some
swā advb	so
swā swā advb	just as
swēte adj	sweet
swīþe, swȳþe advb	very
swiċdom m	betrayal
syn see bēon	
syndan see bēon	
synn f	sin
ġetæl n	story
tēode see tēon	
tēon 1	adorn
tō prep	to
tōcyme m	coming
ġetrēowð f	loyalty
þā advb, conj	then, when

þafian 2	agree to
þanne see þonne	
þanon advb	thence
þās see þis	
þænne see þonne	
þǽr advb, conj	there
þætte conj	that
þe particle	who, which
þēah advb	although
þēaw m	virtue
þēod f	nation
ġeþēodan 1	receive
þēodsċipe m	nation
þes þis þēos demon	this
þēow m	servant
þider, þyder advb	whither
þing n	thing
þinċan 1	seem
þonne advb	then
þū pron	thou
þurh prep	through
þus advb	thus

understandan VI	understand
unlagu f	crime
unriht n	wrong
unsidu m	vice
unðances advb	against the will
up prep	up
uppon prep	upon

wēsten n	wilderness
wǽre see wesan	
wæter n	water
weard advb	towards
weard f	guardian
wedbryċe m	oath-breaking
wel advb	well
wendan 1	go
weorc n	work
weorðan III	become, be
werð see weorðan	
wesan V, see also beon	be
wician 2	stay
wið prep	with

wīde advb	widely
wiðinnan advb	inside
ġewiðūtan advb	outside
wīf n	woman
willa m	will
willan pr-pr	wish, want
witan pr-pr	know
wolde see willan	
word n	word
worhtan see wyrċan	
worold f	world
woruldhād m	secular life
wrītan I	write
wuldorfæder m	father of glory
ġewundian 2	wound
wundor n	wonder
wundra see wundor	
wynsum adj	joyful
wyrsa adj	worse
wyrċan 1	do, make
yfel adj	evil
yfelian 2	worsen
ymbe prep	about

Glossary of linguistic terms

ablaut – the patterned variation of vowel sounds in relation to meaning in forms of the same root; this variation may be in terms either of vowel quality or of vowel duration; it is seen in present-day English in verbs such as *sing* ~ *sang* ~ *sung*.

accusative case – grammatical case usually exhibited by a noun phrase often functioning as the direct object of the verb, and usually (but by no means always) expressing semantically the goal or patient of the action that the verb denotes.

active – see **voice**.

affix – **prefix** or **suffix**.

affixation – process of adding an **affix**.

agreement – formal relation between two elements, so the form of one element is required to correspond with the form of the other.

allomorph – one of the variant pronunciations of a morpheme, among which the choice is determined by context (phonological, grammatical or lexical). For example, [z], [əz] and [s] are phonologically determined allomorphs of the plural suffix, occurring respectively in 'cats', 'dogs' and 'horses'. A morpheme with only one pronunciation is sometimes said to have only one allomorph.

allophone – one or more phonetic variants of the same **phoneme**.

anacrusis – an introductory syllable at the beginning, and preceding, the normal metrical scheme.

Anglo-Norman – the variety of French spoken by those who invaded England at the time of the Norman Conquest, and their descendants.

aspect – the grammatical means which marks the duration or type of temporal activity denoted by the verb; in English we find progressive (*I am sleeping*) and perfective (*I have slept*) aspect.

auxiliary verb – a set of verbs which have primarily grammatical meaning and which are associated with a following lexical verb; a subset of these verbs are called in present-day English modal verbs, but it is not clear that such a subset existed in Old English.

bahuvrihi – another term for **exocentric**, drawn from the terminology of traditional Sanskrit grammarians.

borrowing – see **loan word**.

bound morpheme, bound allomorph – **morpheme** or **allomorph** that cannot stand on its own as a word. A bound morpheme is one whose allomorphs are all bound. See also **free morpheme**.

case – grammatical category expressing the relationship of a noun phrase to the verb in its clause. See also **nominative, accusative, genitive, dative, instrumental**.

cause – the element which is the source of the action or state expressed by the verb.

Celtic – one of the branches of **Indo-European**, from which are descended, amongst others, the present-day languages Breton, Irish Gaelic, Scots Gaelic and Welsh.

clitic – a small word which becomes attached to an adjacent and more important word.

coda – see **syllable**.

cognate – of words, derived from the same historical source. For example, the English word 'father' and the French word 'père' are cognate, both being descended (through Proto-Germanic and Latin respectively) from the same Proto-Indo-European word.

comparison – grammatical category associated with adjectives. Many English adjectives distinguish basic or 'positive', 'comparative' and 'superlative' forms (e.g. *hot, hotter, hottest*).

complementary distribution – see **distribution**.

complementiser – a type of conjunction which is used to mark one clause as dependent on another.

compound – word containing more than one root (or combining form).

concord – see **agreement**.

conjugation – a set of verbs which share the same **paradigm**.

content word – word which has full lexical meaning, see **function word**.

contrastive distribution – see **distribution**.

conversion – the derivation of one **lexeme** from another (e.g. the verb 'father' from the noun 'father') without any overt change in shape. Some linguists analyse this phenomenon as zero-derivation.

coordination – where two syntactic units are linked together with equal status.

correlation – where a pair of structures are linked by parallel element order.

dative – grammatical case usually exhibited by a noun phrase often functioning as the indirect object of the verb.

declension – a set either of nouns or of adjectives which share the same paradigm.

definite ~ indefinite – Old English adjectives had two declensions; where the adjective was preceded by a demonstrative or possessive it followed the definite declension, and elsewhere it followed the indefinite declension.

deixis – a term used to refer to those features which relate to personal, locational or temporal, where meaning is relative to that situation.

derivational morphology – area of morphology concerned with the way in which **lexemes** are related to one another (or in which one lexeme is derived from another) through processes such as **affixation**.

digraph – the combination of two letters to represent a single sound, as in the <th> of *this*.

distribution – in a sound system there are sets of sounds which contrast with each other, and such sounds are said to be in contrastive distribution; there are other sounds with do not contrast but appear in different positions in the word – for example for many speakers of English the first sound in *little* is different from the last sound, but this has no effect on the sound system, because they two sounds are not contrastive, but rather complementary.

dual – see **number**.

endocentric (of a **compound** or derived word) – possessing a **head**. See also **exocentric**.

exocentric (of a **compound** or derived word) – lacking a **head**. For example, the noun *sell-out* is exocentric because it contains no component that determines its word class ('sell' being a verb and 'out' being an adverb).

experiencer – the animate entity affected by the action or state expressed by the verb.

finite – used of verbs which have a subject, hence non-finite verbs lack a subject.

focus – in discourse, the element which is given the most communicative importance.

focussed – a norm to which speakers tend, rather than a fixed standard.

free morpheme, free allomorph – **morpheme** or **allomorph** that can stand on its own as a word. A morpheme may have both free and bound allomorphs, e.g. *wife* is free but *wive-* is bound because it appears only in the plural word form *wives*.

function word – word which has grammatical rather than lexical meaning.

geminate – a double or long consonant, similar to the medial sequence in PDE *hat-trick*.

gender – syntactically and morphologically relevant classification of nouns, present in Old English (as in modern German and French) but lost in modern English. The gender to which an animate noun belongs may be determined by sex, but for most nouns in Old English gender was semantically arbitrary.

genitive – grammatical case usually exhibited by a noun phrase when the phrase is being used in a possessive function.

Germanic – one of the branches of **Indo-European**, from which are descended, amongst others, the present-day languages English, Dutch, Frisian, German, Danish, Icelandic, Norwegian and Swedish.

government – process by which one phrase has control over another, for example a verb may determine the case assigned to an object.

gradation, qualitative and quantitative – see **ablaut**.

head – element within a **compound** or derived word that determines the syntactic status, or word class, of the whole word. Semantically, also, a compound noun whose head is X usually denotes a type of X. For example, 'house' is the head of the compound 'greenhouse'. Many linguists would also analyse some derivational affixes as heads, e.g. -*er* as the head of the noun 'teacher'.

homophone – two words which are identical in pronunciation, for example *know* and *no*.

hypotaxis – where one syntactic unit is linked to another by means of **subordination**.

iambic pentameter – metrical verse form where each line is based upon a template of five feet, each consisting of an unstressed syllable followed by a stressed syllable; naturally almost all poets vary the form of the line.

imperative – see **mood**.

indicative – see **mood**.

Indo-European – the language family from which are descended not only the Germanic languages, but a very wide range of languages throughout Europe and many parts of the Middle East and Indian sub-continent.

infinitive – usually taken as the basic or unmarked non-finite verbal form.

infinitive, inflected – special form of the Old English **infinitive** which occurs when governed by the preposition *tō*.

inflectional morphology – area of morphology concerned with changes in word shape (e.g. through **affixation**) that are determined by, or potentially affect, the grammatical context in which a word appears. See also **lexeme**.

instrumental – a **case** used when the noun phrase exhibits functions such as 'association with', but such functions often shown by the dative rather than the instrumental. The instrumental is also used in a variety of idiomatic expressionism.

language family – a set of languages which are **cognate**, as in the case of Indo-European.

lexeme – word seen as an abstract grammatical entity, represented concretely by one or more different inflected word forms according to the grammatical context. For example, the verb lexeme 'perform' has four inflected word forms: 'perform', 'performs', 'performing' and 'performed'.

lexicon – inventory of lexical items, seen as part of a native speaker's knowledge of his or her language.

loan word – a word from another language which is taken into English.

macron – a mark placed above a vowel by editors in order to show that the vowel is long.

mood – a set of semantic contrasts signalling the attitudes of the speaker and in Old English shown by three different moods, indicative, subjunctive and imperative.

modal verb – see **auxiliary verb**.

morpheme – minimal unit of grammatical structure. (The morpheme is often defined as the minimal meaningful unit of language but that definition leads to problems, as explained in Section 3.5.)

morphology – area of grammar concerned with the structure of words and with relationships between words that involve the **morphemes** that compose them.

mutation – see **umlaut**.

negative concord – negation falls not only on a verb phrase but also on any other appropriate element in the clause, as in non-standard present-day English *I didn't see nothing.*

nominal – belonging to the word class 'noun', or having the characteristics of a noun.

nominative case – grammatical case exhibited by a noun phrase functioning as the subject of the verb, and usually (but by no means always) expressing semantically the agent of the action that the verb denotes.

nucleus – see **syllable**.

number – grammatical category associated especially with nouns. In English, 'plural' and 'singular' numbers are distinguished inflectionally (e.g. 'cats' versus 'cat'). In Old English there was also a dual category, occasionally used with pronouns and adjectives.

onset – see **syllable**.

orthography – the spelling system of a language.

parataxis – where two syntactic units are linked together by juxtaposition and without any conjunction.

passive – see **voice**.

paradigm – the set of forms associated with a noun or an adjective in forming a declensional class, or with a verb in a conjugational class.

past – see **tense**.

person – grammatical category associated especially with pronouns, identifying individuals in relation to the speaker and hearer. English distinguishes 'first person' (I, we), 'second person' (you) and 'third person' (he, she, it, they).

phoneme – the minimal unit in the sound system of a language. Collectively, the contrasting sounds in any given language.

phonology – area of grammar concerned with how speech sounds function to distinguish words in a language (and in languages generally). The scope of phonology includes how sounds are related, how they are combined to form syllables and larger units, and how relationships between syllables are indicated by features such as stress.

prefix – **bound morpheme** that immediately precedes the root or **stem**.

present – see **tense**.

preterite – a morphological form usually expressing past tense.

plural – see **number**.

prefix – **bound morpheme** that precedes the root or **stem**.

register – the varieties of language used in particular social situations, for example formal vs. colloquial.

relative particle – an element which has the function of a **complementiser** used to introduce a relative clause.

resolution – the feature in Old English poetry where two light **syllables** have the same effect as one heavy syllable.

schwa – the reduced vowel found, for example, in the first syllable of 'about' or the last syllable of 'butter'.

singular – see **number**.

standard language – an regularised and institutionalised variety of a language used in administration, education, etc.; see also **focussed**.

stem – term used for the base of the word forms of a **lexeme** (involving the addition of inflectional **affixes** only, not derivational ones).

stranding – when an element is left unattached to or moved out of its construction.

subjunctive – see **mood**.

subordination – where one syntactic unit is dependent upon another.

suffix – **bound morpheme** that follows the root or **stem**.

suffixoid – an element which shares the properties of a **suffix** and an independent word, and whose morphological status is therefore uncertain.

suppletion – phenomenon whereby one **lexeme** is represented by two or more different roots, depending on the context; for example, the verb 'go' is represented by 'went' in the past tense and 'go' elsewhere.

syllable – consists of a vowel and its immediately preceding and following consonants; hence onset describes the preceding consonant(s) and coda the following ones, while the central vowel element(s) are the nucleus.

syncope – the loss of an unstressed vowel.

tense – grammatical category exhibited by verbs, closely associated with time. In English, a distinction between present and past tenses is expressed inflectionally, e.g. 'give' and 'wait' versus 'gave' and 'waited'.

umlaut – an historical process by which back vowels were fronted and front vowels raised; the change is most easily observed in nouns such as *foot* ~ *feet*.

velar – a sound produced by moving the back of the tongue against the soft palate or velum.

verb, contracted – a verb where the final consonant of the **stem** (preceding any inflection) has been lost.

verb, preterite-present – a verb where the past tense has acquired a new present tense meaning, with the subsequent acquisition of a new set of past tense forms.

verb, inseparable, separable – where a prefix may either always remain with the **stem** against prefixes which may be separated from their stem by a variety of elements and word order type.

verb, weak and strong – the two major morphological groups of verbs in Old English; the former relate to present-day verbs such as *love*, the latter to verbs like *sing*.

Verner's Law – the series of changes in stops and fricatives which distinguish Germanic from most of Indo-European languages, first discovered by Karl Verner.

voice – the means by which relationships between the subject and the object are expressed, hence the categories active and passive.

weight – the amount of phonological material contained in a word.

word-formation – the process of creating new words by means of either affixation or compounding.

word order – sequence in which words occur; of particular interest in Old English is the position of the verb.

zero – a **morpheme** which contains no phonological elements.

Recommended reading

I have chosen to present the recommended reading in sections here, rather than at the end of each chapter, since I believe this will prove more helpful, allowing you to contextualise your reading more easily. It will also allow a more coherent understanding of how the different parts of Old English fit together.

1 General histories

There are very many histories of the English language, but amongst the most widely used, Barber (1993) and Baugh and Cable (2002) are both very accessible at this level. Two other works at the same level which are particularly useful for their illustrative material although less full on many relevant details are Freeborn (1998) and Graddol (1996). Another excellent work which covers both the Old and the Middle English period, with a slightly wider selection of texts is Smith (1999). In the same series as this book, Smith and his colleague Simon Horobin have written the companion volume on Middle English (Horobin & Smith 2002).

Of more advanced general histories, by far the best remains Strang (1970). It is both sophisticated and readable, with many powerful insights. It is to be hoped that the forthcoming *History of the English Language* (Hogg & Denison 2003) will show some of the best from Strang's work as well as offering a necessary update. Two other books which proved stimulating reading are Lass (1987) and Smith (1996). If you wish to proceed further then the multi-volume *The Cambridge History of the English Language* is essential (Hogg 1992–2001).

2 Old English

By far the best short grammar of Old English is Quirk and Wrenn (1957), still widely available in libraries. Its principal shortcomings are the absence of any texts and the fact that it is rather outdated. Nevertheless it is an invaluable supplement to this present work. The most used Old English textbook is Mitchell and Robinson (2001), now in its sixth edition. It has an excellent set of texts of all types and is hardly likely to be superseded in the foreseeable future. Despite the authority of its editors, it is somewhat marred, from our point of view, by its idiosyncratic style and a perceptibly 'anti-linguistic' approach. Beyond these two works the most interesting book must be Lass (1994), which leads any reader into a wealth of material.

In terms of grammars as such, however, there no few good grammar books about Old English which lie between the level of Quirk and Wrenn and the more detailed handbooks such as Brunner (1965), Campbell (1959), Girvan (1931) and Hogg (1992), which cannot be recommended for anyone other than a specialist. Furthermore all of these works concentrate on Old English phonology and morphology only, reflected in their traditional use of the term *grammar*. The best available intermediate grammar is probably Pilch (1970), a German work. Another German work which was well-received when it was published was the generative analysis of Wagner (1969). It is now seriously outdated and it is regrettable that there has never been a comparable later work. Another early generative work which remains interesting although also outdated is Lass and Anderson (1975).

There are a large number of collections of texts which might be mentioned, but they are largely redundant given the presence of Mitchell and Robinson. But for anyone who wishes to go further, then the next step forward is *Sweet's Anglo-Saxon Reader* (Whitelock 1967).

3 Phonology

Although I have tried to omit as much phonological discussion as possible in this text, there are many works which are widely available. A first-class introduction to English phonology can be found in McMahon (2002), a companion to this work. A work which many, especially perhaps non-native, readers will be familiar with is that by A. C. Gimson on the pronunciation of English, which contains a short discussion of Old English. This work is now in its sixth edition, having been revised by Alan Cruttenden (Cruttenden 2001). North American readers, and others too, may find Ladefoged (1993), although neither historical nor merely concerned with English, an essential guide.

More advanced works on phonology which have good material on English include Giegerich (1992), Jones (1989) and Lass (1984). Many of the works mentioned in §2 devote most of, sometimes even all, their time to phonological issues. Many of the phonological issues I have covered here derive from my own work in Hogg (1992)

4 Morphology

In morphology it is customary, although not essential, to distinguish between inflection morphology and derivational morphology, and I have adopted that approach here. A very useful work which appears in the same series as this work and which includes a section on the historical sources of present-day English morphological formations is Carstairs-McCarthy (2002). See also §6 below for derivational morphology and other issues relating to vocabulary.

In other respects most of the works concerning morphology have been cited already in §3, especially Quirk and Wrenn (1957). Others will be found in §6. But good general textbooks include Bauer (1988) and, above all, the quite difficult but essential and sophisticated Matthews (1991) are recommended for anyone who wishes to pursue the subject further. The present work is based on my own study (Hogg 1992), mentioned in §3.

5 Syntax

As I have said, most of the handbooks cited in §2 have very little on Old English syntax and only Quirk and Wrenn (1957) can be safely recommended for the beginner. At the next stage perhaps the most useful material is to be found in the general histories of English cited in §1. For anyone who needs a beginner's guide to present-day English syntax, a helpful source is the companion volume Miller (2002).

For more advanced work on Old English syntax, Denison (1993) offers an excellent overview and discussion of both current and earlier work. This work also brings a fresh perspective not only to Old English but also to the later syntactic history of the language. It is very densely written work, and you should probably skip areas in which you are not directly interested. Beyond that stage you will need to look at the important and useful essay by Traugott (1992) in the *Cambridge History*. The most authoritative work on Old English syntax is undoubtedly the two-volume work by Mitchell (1985), but even for the most advanced reader this is by no means an easy work. If you use it at all, then use it as a reference work, to be consulted only for essential matters of detail. A further advanced work which deals all of the history of English syntax, not merely Old English, is the standard work of Visser (1963–73), which is essential for the most advanced students.

6 Vocabulary

As with phonology and syntax, there is a companion volume in this series on English morphology, namely Carstairs-McCarthy (2002). This has a good, if necessarily brief, overview of the relevant issues. To some extent its approach is slightly different from that pursued, but the comparison should be interesting.

The Old English handbooks rarely have much to offer on either loan words or derivational morphology, but for the latter Quirk and Wrenn (1957) remains essential. One recent work of very great importance here is Stockwell and Minkova (2001). Beyond that, the standard text for loan words throughout the history of English remains Serjeantson (1935), despite its age. It is not too difficult to read, especially in conjunction with the standard histories of the language. A more detailed account of both vocabulary and word formation is to be found in the more technical essay by Kastovsky in the *Cambridge History* (Kastovsky 1992).

In terms of dictionaries, the most accessible Old English dictionary is Clark

Hall and Merritt (1969). The major Old English dictionary, namely Bosworth and Toller (1898) and Toller (1921), cannot be used except with extreme care, for reasons Toller clearly explains in his introductory remarks. The major new *Dictionary of Old English* is being compiled at Toronto, parts of it are now available. Another dictionary which is, of course, essential is *The Oxford English Dictionary*, the second edition of which is available on CD-ROM as well as in traditional book form.

7 Poetry

If you can find a copy, by far the easiest place to start any investigation of Old English metrical structure, is with the description of Old English verse by Tolkien in Clark Hall, Wrenn and Tolkien (1950), but it is probably only to be found in libraries or second-hand bookshops. Tolkien imaginatively and brilliantly shows how such a verse might operate in present-day English.

The foundations of Old English metre were laid by Eduard Sievers (1893). An updated version of Sievers' work was published by Bliss (1958). Old English metre remains a controversial area, and therefore anyone interested in the subject should also examine Cable (1974).

8 Variation

There is at present no satisfactory account of Old English dialect variation other than that found in the standard handbooks and the older works upon which they are largely based. The only full-length modern, sociolinguistically based, approach is that found in Toon (1983), but that work must be used with care.

9 Linguistic change

A good introductory text for anyone with little or no knowledge of the subject is the very readable Aitchison (2001). There are so many introductions to historical linguistics that the choice may be a matter of taste. However a well-established work which has particular interests in Indo-European and Germanic is Lehmann (1992). Two other good works are Campbell (1998) and McMahon (1994). Many of the standard histories mentioned above also have good accounts of the pre-history of English. For a much more advanced, and individual, account of the issues, Lass (1997) is very stimulating and again has a great deal about Germanic. But if any of you wish to pursue in a little more detail the comparisons between Old English and its closest relatives, then the place to start is undoubtedly Robinson (1992).

References

Aitchison, Jean (1991), *Language Change: progress or decay?* (2nd edn), Cambridge: Cambridge University Press.

Barber, Charles L. (1993), *The English Language: a historical introduction*, Cambridge: Cambridge University Press.

Bauer, Laurie (1988), *Introducing Linguistic Morphology*, Edinburgh: Edinburgh University Press.

Baugh, Albert C. and Thomas Cable (2002), *A History of the English Language* (5th edn), London: Routledge.

Bliss, Alan J. (1958), *The Metre of Beowulf*, Oxford: Basil Blackwell.

Brunner, Karl (1965), *Altenglische Grammatik* (3rd edn), Tübingen: Max Niemeyer.

Cable, Thomas (1974), *The Meter and Melody of Beowulf*, Urbana, IL: University of Illinois.

Campbell, Alistair (1959), *Old English Grammar*, Oxford: Clarendon Press.

Campbell, Lyle (1998), *Historical Linguistics: an introduction*, Edinburgh: Edinburgh University Press.

Carstairs-McCarthy, Andrew (2002), *An Introduction to English Morphology*, Edinburgh: Edinburgh University Press.

Clark Hall, John R. and Herbert D. Merrit (1969), *A Concise Anglo-Saxon Dictionary* (4th edn), Cambridge: Cambridge University Press.

Clark Hall, John R., Charles R. Wrenn and J. R. R. Tolkien (1950), *Beowulf and the Finnesburg Fragment*, London: Allen and Unwin.

Cruttenden, Alan (2001), *Gimson's Pronunciation of English* (6th edn), London: Edward Arnold.

Denison, David (1993), *English Historical Syntax*, London: Longman.

Freeborn, Dennis (1998), *From Old English to Standard English* (2nd edn), Basingstoke: Macmillan.

Giegerich, Heinz J. (1992), *English Phonology: an introduction*, Cambridge: Cambridge University Press.

Girvan, R. (1931), *Angelsaksisch Handboek*, Haarlem: Tjeenk Willink.

Graddol, David, Dick Leith and Joan Swann (1996), *English: history, diversity and change*, London: Routledge.

Hogg, Richard M. (1992), *The Cambridge History of the English Language*. Vol. 1, Cambridge: Cambridge University Press.

Hogg, Richard M. (1992), *A Grammar of Old English*, Oxford: Basil Blackwell.

Hogg, Richard M. (1992), 'Phonology', in R. M. Hogg (ed.), *The Cambridge History of the English Language*, Cambridge: Cambridge University Press, pp. 67–167.

Hogg, Richard M. and David Denison (2003), *A History of the English Language*, Cambridge: Cambridge University Press.

Horobin, Simon and Jeremy J. Smith (2002), *An Introduction to Middle English*, Edinburgh: Edinburgh University Press.

Kastovsky, Dieter (1992), 'Semantics and vocabulary', in R. M. Hogg (ed.), *The Cambridge History of the English Language*, Cambridge: Cambridge University Press, pp. 290–408.

Ladefoged, Peter (1993), *A Course in Phonetics* (2nd edn), Fort Worth, TX: Harcourt Brace.

Lass, Roger (1984), *Phonology: an introduction to basic concepts*, Cambridge: Cambridge University Press.

Lass, Roger (1987), *The Shape of English*, London: Dent.

Lass, Roger (1994), *Old English: an historical linguistic companion*, Cambridge: Cambridge University Press.

Lass, Roger (1997), *Historical Linguistics and Language Change*, Cambridge: Cambridge University Press.

Lass, Roger and John Anderson (1975), *Old English Phonology*, Cambridge: Cambridge University Press.

Matthews, Peter H. (1991), *Morphology* (2nd edn), Cambridge: Cambridge University Press.

McMahon, April (2002), *An Introduction to English Phonology*, Edinburgh: Edinburgh University Press.

McMahon, April M. S. (1994), *Understanding Language Change*, Cambridge: Cambridge University Press.

Miller, Jim (2002), *An Introduction to English Syntax*, Edinburgh: Edinburgh University Press.

Mitchell, Bruce (1985), *Old English Syntax*, 2 vols, Oxford: Clarendon Press.

Mitchell, R. Bruce and Fred C. Robinson (1992), *A Guide to Old English* (6th edn), Oxford: Blackwell.

Pitch, Herbert (1970), *Altenglische Grammatik*, München: Max Hueber Verlag.

Quirk, Randolph and Charles L. Wrenn (1957), *An Old English Grammar* (2nd edn), London: Methuen.

Robinson, Orrin W. (1992), *Old English and Its Closest Relatives*, Stanford, CA: Stanford University Press.

Smith, Jeremy J. (1996), *An Historical Study of English*, London: Routledge.

Stockwell, Robert P. and Donka Minkova (2001), *English Words: history and structure*, Cambridge: Cambridge University Press.

Strang, Barbara Mary Hope (1970), *A History of English*, London: Methuen.

Toller, Thomas Northcote (1921), *An Anglo-Saxon Dictionary: Supplement*, Oxford: Oxford University Press.

Traugott, Elizabeth Closs (1992), 'Syntax', in R. M. Hogg (ed.), *The Cambridge History of the English Language, I: the beginnings to 1066*, Cambridge: Cambridge

University Press, pp. 168–289.

Visser, F. T. (1963–73), *An Historical Syntax of the English Language*, Leiden: E. J. Brill.

Wagner, Karl Heinz (1969), *Generative Grammatical Studies in the Old English language*, Heidelberg: Julius Groos.

Whitelock, Dorothy (1967), *Sweet's Anglo-Saxon Reader*, Oxford: Clarendon Press.

Index